GOING WEST AIN'T EASY GOING

GOING WEST AIN'T EASY GOING

Ivo Moravec

Copyright © 2017 Ivo Moravec

All rights reserved. This book or any portion thereof may not be reproduced or used in any manner whatsoever without the express written permission of the publisher except for the use of brief quotations in a book review.

moravecbooks@gmail.com

First Printing, 2017
ISBN 978-0-9949128-2-4

In memory of my Dad, Jaroslav

Table of Contents

Lucerna Hall or Prologue 1
On the Road 6
Chotouň in Colorado 8
Horse thieves 11
Sainte-Marie among the Huron 13
Alcatraz 16
Happy Destiny 19
Beer in Pennsylvania 21
Terra sacra 23
Boot Hills 26
Monte Vegas 28
The High After Noon 32
Weekend in Fredonia 34
Whistler 40
Singer Heritage 42
Birch Canoe 45
Big Canoe 49
Manitou's Backyard 51
Low Tide 53
Satellite Dishes 55
Two pubs 57
Nautilus 60
Cody 62
Kennedy Space Centre 65
Guanella Pass 68
No Name Wonders 73
Green Province 75
Air Density 77

Do You Speak BMW?	78
Temples	80
everyday poetry	82
Labrador	84
Scribner's	86
Pine tree	89
Workhorses	91
Davenport	93
Moose	95
Prairie Campground	98
Mess Tin	100
Edwards	102
Golf Plots	106
Monsieur Breton Would Smile	109
Blueberry Art	110
Changing of the Guard	111
Bonneville	113
Los Angeles Tangent	115
The Land's End	117
Exotics	119
Crossing Northern Iowa	121
City Lights	123
Fraction of Rivers	127
Street Performers	128
Aboard the Ferry	130
Mount Rushmore	133
Encounter Among the Remainder Books	135
In Canadian Utah	138
Rebellion in North Dakota	140
Roaring Fork	143

Oregon Trail 145

Downside of Being Big 147

Hats 149

Athabasca 151

Monument Valley 154

Islands and Hydroplanes 156

Canyon to Precambrian 158

Waffle House 160

Snapshot in the Kootenays 162

Mystery Spots or New Prague 164

Original Oranges 167

Sequoias 169

Soul Travelling 173

Mr O or Epilogue 175

Lucerna Hall or Prologue

Encore, encore, encore, chanted the pumped up crowd in the Lucerna Hall, the venerable Prague venue for pop music concerts. Little did the audience know that the song they were about to hear, would turn this concert from memorable to unforgettable, even legendary.

Sitting in the audience, Mr. Leopold Korbař, the composer of the melody of this never-quite-hit-evergreen, shivered. His life experience told him, right after the first bar, that the proverbial excrement was dangerously close to the fan and about to hit. He was sure about the disaster when the whole Hall roared in response to the first line of lyric:

Going West ain't easy going
and somebody shouted: "Never mind, we've got young legs..."
The audience caught up and, beside singing along, started to answer the singer
The grass has overgrown the trail
"so what, we'll mow it down..."
In vain I search for the right path
"as long as it leads to the West..."
Calling my name, the West robs me of sleep
"so, jump out of bed, dummy, and start running..."

That scandal spelled a long pause in the public appearances of the Prague Syncopated Orchestra, a revivalist big band that played songs from the era when musicians performed well dressed, in tuxedos and bow ties, from the swing era, in the original arrangements and authentic style of singing. The lyrics for this contentious song were written by my Dad in 1938. The song was the first collaboration of two twenty year old jazz fans and was titled *Going West Ain't Easy Going*. In its days, it was one of the so-called Cowboy songs, so the long and difficult journey of the title probably meant the long wagon trails across the prairies of the American Midwest.

Within a year of the song's publication, the Nazis rolled into Czechoslovakia. In accordance with their paradigm, they understood the word West in the political rather than the geographical sense. The West was the enemy. Going West meant defection. The song was banned, but it survived the six years of the occupation without being completely forgotten. After the war, it was played again, gained decent popularity and might have been on the way to becoming an evergreen. The word evergreen is commonly used in Czech for songs that don't fade into oblivion, but retain their popularity over decades.

Then the communists grabbed the power and, in accordance with their paradigm, once again understood the word "West" in the political rather than the geographical sense. The West was the enemy. Going West meant defection. The song was banned. Still, it survived, unforgotten, twenty more years till the political thaw of the Prague spring in 1968 when, occasionally, it resurfaced. With the re-freezing after the Russian military invasion and occupation, the song was put on ice again, presumably to prevent its lyrics from encouraging people to emigrate.

In the meantime, the song became more popular than ever, as so often happens to forbidden fruit, as Eve herself could testify. It became a folk song of sorts, being played and sung at camp fires, country pubs, places where the reach of the authorities was weaker. That's why the Lucerna Hall audience knew the lyrics. Of course, the musicians were aware that it was banned, but in 1982 they might have gotten away with playing it, if not for that reaction of the audience. Taking their cue from the authorities, the audience also saw "West" in political rather than geographical terms, at least in the context of this periodically banned song. Well, the fate might have been much worse for the orchestra than a few years of prohibition to perform in public or to be broadcast over the mass media. Mr. Korbař received an indefinite, long term 'suspension' as well, though, in his case, being a mere spectator, having nothing to do with the performance, he'd been perfectly innocent.

I don't know for how long this suspension was enforced. The following year I myself succumbed to the call of the West – both political and geographical - defected with my family to Austria and from there emigrated to Canada. Since then I have had plenty of opportunities to verify how long and arduous that journey, that going West, really is.

Today, the song is more than seventy years old and is not only alive but thriving, having regained its popularity again after the fall of communism in Czechoslovakia. Dad would have been very happy.

Why should a cowboy song be written and become popular in Czechoslovakia in the first place, you may ask. There were no cowboys, no Wild West, in Bohemia. The West has not been a part of Czech folklore. Fair question.

In the early nineteen twenties, a new social trend began to take shape in Bohemia. Without ever reading J. J. Rousseau, a number of people were practising *retour à la Nature*. From spring to fall, every Saturday noon, as soon as the buzzer announced the end of their shift, young people grabbed backpacks and tents, ran to the railway station, jumped on bicycles or into canoes, and pedalled or paddled twenty or forty kilometres outside their cities, into a forest, or the bank of a pond, a river, a creek - just about anywhere among trees would do. They spent Saturday evening shooting the breeze with friends around a campfire, slept in a tent or under the stars. Sunday was a day of rest and leisure. They might go picking wild mushrooms or blueberries, swim, sunbathe, play volleyball, or simply be lazy. In the evening they returned to the cities. Those brief escapes from everyday greyness were their little touches of poetry. They called it *tramping*, though the precise English meaning was misunderstood. Camping would be closer to what they practised. The imagination of this movement was fed on travel memoirs, exploration accounts and adventure books, from good authors like Jack London, E. T. Seton, and James Curwood to dozens of their epigones. The first Western movies with Tom Mix and other gunslingers were added to the mix. Mass produced paperbacks of pulp cowboy fiction found their readers too.

A country as densely populated as Czechoslovakia can have no real wilderness. That's one reason why America, with no distinction made between Canada and the US, simply America from Mexico to Alaska, dreamed of, unfamiliar, but uncompromisingly idealized and mythologized, became the most romantic, the most promised land, the ultimate paradise of the tough outdoorsman and adventurer. Wilderness was the subject of talks around campfires, the theme of songs strummed on a guitar. The popular song *Plaintive Humming of Niagara* was written by a man who wouldn't see the Falls until some twenty years later. Sort of embryonic country and western music, Czech style.

My Dad, university student at that time, wasn't a fan of this wandering about in the woods, though he was a fan of America. In his case, he was fascinated by the way Louis Armstrong blew his cornet and Benny Goodman his clarinet, by the wizardry of Chick Webb on drums and Duke Ellington on piano, and, most of all, the way Glenn Miller made his big band swing. For him, America meant jazz, and in his day jazz meant big band swing.

Revolutionary music. The opposite of brass bands rolling out the barrels of polkas and waltzes that ruled Czech popular music at the time, jazz was an index of the generational divide in Bohemia. He begun to write lyrics, and, later, occasionally, music too. Within two years he was a hit maker. A long list of songs with his lyrics became Czech evergreens. Neither under the Nazis nor the Communists, of course, was his career an easy one. For both regimes jazz was degenerate music to be tolerated at best, and, at worst, actively suppressed. After the war, he extended his interests to include American movies and radio broadcast plays. He was borrowing the latter, in book form, in the library of the American embassy in Prague until the library was closed down. He never travelled to America, never saw America in person. Fate, in the form of communists, prevented that. He passed away in 1954, so I will never know what images of America swing music conjured in his mind, what kind of America he imagined on the basis of movies and plays. I can only guess how much his images would overlap with reality. Reconciling the images with reality, no easy and quick task, was left to me, the emigrant. But today I can see that, owing to his artistic intuition, Dad's guess was right on: going West ain't easy going. Especially, when it comes to Western thinking. Believe me. Ain't easy.

* * * * * *

On the Road

To keep rolling and rolling down the road can be exhilarating. I understood that at once, right at the beginning of our first trip to the West, long before we could make it anywhere famous and see anything of renown. An hour or two after crossing border on the bridge between Sarnia and Port Huron in Michigan, we were rolling through green forests.

My wife Jana and son Ivo occupied the two remaining captain's chairs in this old Ford cargo van that we refurbished as a simple camper. You won't read much about Jana and Ivo in the following pages though they have both brought a great deal to all those stories. Not only have we done all the travelling together, but as a closely knit family we've always shared our thoughts, insights and feelings. After thirty plus years of our marriage it would be very difficult to draw the precise boundary line between Jana's mind and my own to specify who contributed what to the shared experience. Presenting the stories in the first person, consistently using the same I, allows me to keep the storytelling simple, to write from a single point of view, with a single voice, fully focused on what I, or we, wish to share. *And* Jana and Ivo are quite happy to be present as parts of "we".

Far away ahead, straight along the line of the freeway, the huge red ball of the setting sun marked the direction of our travels.

We knew that ahead of us was an almost endless journey, a series of journeys, always heading West, all the way to British Columbia or California, west, west, until we would be stopped by a sign, erected on a high cliff above the Pacific – End of the Road.

This huge, unknown, anticipated and as yet unexplored continent in front of the windscreen doesn't make you apprehensive or fearful of the unknown. Not only does it attract and fascinate you, it floods you with an unbelievable feeling of freedom. It's up to you and only you to decide what you wish to see and where you wish to go. It's up to you how much you push the gas pedal and where you turn your steering wheel. You literally have the direction and destination of your travels in your own hands. In front of you nothing but West is waiting – near West, mid West, wild West, far West - and anything you wish to pick up from it, to savour with your sight, touch, hearing, smell and taste, is yours. You're floating, almost choking with delight just imagining the mental feasts awaiting you. You feel infinitely rich, regardless of how thin the wad of dollars in your pocket might be. Let's roll! Straight ahead. Anywhere you head, an adventure is waiting. Just charging down a freeway in a free country is intoxicating – you're right Mr. Kerouac. Let's roooollll!

Chotouň in Colorado

Did you climb trees in your childhood? I did. Especially two massive cherry trees growing in the garden of the family country house in the hamlet called Chotouň. Chotouň – the magic place of my childhood. An old country house surrounded by an acre of land, bought years ago by my grandfather, was a leisure place for the whole family, his three married daughters and their children, my cousins. There we spent all the weekends and, of course, all our vacations.

I think you'll agree that a cherry picked from its stem on a branch high on the tree and popped into your mouth right away, tastes different from the cherry bought in a store. Especially when you can't buy the variety we had, not in any store. Our cherries were something extra special. Even today I don't know their official name. Folks called them 'crunchies' and they were quite rare in Bohemia. Common cherries called Bing in English are very dark red and much juicier. Ours were coloured from yellow to red, only the most ripe were crimson. They were not particularly juicy but sweet, bigger than the Bings. My cousins and myself started climbing the trees to get them when we were about nine or ten. They started to ripen just as vacations began and took about a month for all of them to turn red.

We were often up that tree, several times each day, sometime just because we felt like a few cherries or sometime acting on the request of grandma who wanted to make cherry dumplings. We used no basket, naturally. That would hamper the climbing. Pick up a fistful of cherries, toss them inside your T-shirt. Eat a few, too - that goes without saying, there's plenty of cherries all around. When my older cousin and myself each had about three pounds of them in our T-shirts, we'd climb down to unload them on grandma's kitchen counter, the dough ready. My mouth still waters when I recall those cherry dumplings – the unforgettable meal of my childhood summers.

Now and then we climbed the tree not so much for the cherries as for a few moments of solitude. Sitting in high branches is very conducive to day dreaming, as if that perch, almost touching the skies, insulated from the earth and earthiness, were a crow's nest on a tall ship - dreaming about reading: the Wild West, the wilderness around the Colorado river, Apaches waging wars with Sioux, wolves in Alaska, grizzlies in the Canadian Rockies, mustangs and buffaloes thundering all over the prairies, blizzards burying the Hudson's Bay outposts and gold prospectors' tents. It wasn't difficult to imagine that a recently tamed mustang was waiting under the tree for me. As soon as I climbed down, I could mount it and ride into a mountain valley full of fragrant pine forest and rich adventure.

Emigration meant parting with many things, cherries among them. During fifteen years of living in Canada and travelling in the US, I haven't found them anywhere else. And I was always looking for them. I missed them. I could occasionally find Bing cherries, the dark red ones, but never the 'crunchies'. Not until our travels brought us to the town of Singleton, or it might have been Shawnee or Bailey, I'm not sure, high in the Rockies above Denver. A small town, a huge superstore where we went from the nearby campground to buy supplies for a day of rest after our two day non-stop drive from Ontario. Walking through that big, brightly lit store I caught a glimpse of them. They looked almost the same as the ones in Chotouň. I picked some up. The same touch, the same smell. I tasted one. Yes! The very same taste! What are they doing here? Must be local produce. What does a 2000 meter above sea level town in Colorado have in common with the 200 meters elevation of Chotouň? Who cares! Having scooped up a fistful I stopped myself at the last moment from tossing them inside my T-shirt. I bought quite a few, enough even for making dumplings, though dumplings might be somewhat hard to make and cook on a campfire.

Back at the campsite, I searched for an appropriate tree to climb to enjoy the cherries in style, but the elevation offered me only pines and spruces and, as you might recall, those are hard to climb. Beside, I am no teenager any more, and after fifty the body flexibility isn't what it used to be. I settled for a picnic table where I enjoyed them one by one. You don't spit out the pits. Oh no, you squeeze them between thumb and crooked forefinger and shoot them into the distance. Ten points if you hit the fire-pit.

The taste of each cherry took away a year of my age and at the same time, branch by branch, lifted higher until I was ten years old again, sitting in the very top of the cherry tree in Chotouň. I was no longer day-dreaming about Colorado; I was in Colorado, and in Chotouň at the same time, and, most importantly, I was in the unexplored valley I had dreamed of, the mountain valley full of fragrant evergreens and adventures waiting for me at each step. Don't tell me time travel doesn't exist.

Horse Thieves

Good guys rode the white horses, bad guys the black ones, women had mares or mules, toddlers were born with spurs on their heels. Saying this, I'm not claiming that everybody knew how to ride a horse, just that there were plenty of horses. Maybe horses weren't exactly cheap, but when a good guy happened to be momentarily without, he could always borrow one, he could ride out onto the prairie, find a herd of wild mustangs, throw a lasso over the neck of its Mr. Universe stallion or a Beauty Queen mare, drag the beast into a corral, break it, tame it, ride it. As a good guy, he was a champion at those skills. In short, the West was full of horses. So I found it rather strange when, reading some western story, I came across the sentence: "You know the law, stranger. You steal a horse, you forfeit your life". Or something to that effect. A bit too much, isn't it? Paying for a horse with your life? I've read about the offer of a kingdom for a horse, but never of life. Considering the plentiful supply, it's a bit off, isn't it?

It took about forty years to make the right connections in my mind. Slow on the uptake, they call it. Almost as slow as the progress of a traveller across the prairies. The prairies are endless. To cross Nebraska, Kansas, or Wyoming takes for ever. The Canadian prairies are even larger and less inhabited. Mind you, you are doing a hundred and have 200 tireless horses under the hood.

Driving west along the I-70 from Grand Junction in Colorado, entering Utah, you suddenly see a big blue sign: *Fill up. The last gas station. No services for 106 miles.* Pardon me? A freeway, an Interstate, without gas stations and stores? Aren't we in America? So you fill her up and enter a wildly picturesque landscape, kind of primeval; lots of red rock hills, outcroppings, boulders, red sand, cracks of canyons, half canyons and mini-canyons. Only rarely do you spot in all that red a green clump or two of vegetation. Rather a user-unfriendly kind of landscape. Even the occasional clouds in the blue skies look darkly menacing and grumpy. And when they release a short heavy rainfall and the whole land is freshly washed and glistening with wetness, you start feeling that what you're seeing might have the look of the Earth on the day when the Lord parted the waters and the dry land. No sign of anything alive.

Of course, sooner or later, an idea crosses your mind: I would hate to have a flat tire out here. Or even any trouble with the horses under the hood. And this is the very moment when something clicks in your mind. With a forty-year delay. Anything alive would have a hard time surviving here. Even in our times, let alone a hundred and fifty years ago. Riding a horse gave a traveller a chance to make it through here before he ran out of food or water, but without a horse... to walk, stagger, then just crawl... How far can a person walk, crawl, in a day? Around here, not only in this neck of the rocks, but anywhere in the prairies, it's awfully far from the middle of one nowhere to the middle of another. You can't travel without a horse, ergo stealing a horse equals murder. And because one doesn't steal a horse in the heat of passion or in self defence or by accident, it's murder premeditated or in the first degree. Consequently, if some such thieving sleazebag protested that his life for the theft of a horse would be a barbaric price, he could be told with clear conscience: for a horse it might be, but around here it's life for life.

Sainte-Marie among the Huron

When I encountered this word combination, in reality a local name, for the first time, I found it somewhat inappropriate, the kind of juxtaposition that surrealist poets dream about. Immediately it conjured in my mind the picture of Michelangelo's Pietà from St. Peter's in Rome. I could see in detail the very young looking, infinitely sad face of the Christ's Mother. Many years ago, I had had the rare pleasure of sitting about ten feet from the original of that statue. Looking at her for a long time. It was one of the most powerful art experiences of my life. Maybe that's why she was the first one now to emerge from the crowd of renaissance Madonnas. Anyway, the impact of this local name on my mind transported the off-white marble statue from the Vatican into the wild trees and bristling bushes on the shores of Lake Huron. Surrounded by the natives with faces covered in war paint, shaking spears and tomahawks and yelling with blood curdling ferocity.

I think you'll agree that a place with such a name is impossible to resist, not to visit, regardless of what you might find there. What you do find is a restored Jesuit mission from the early seventeenth century. Jesuit? Unwelcome news! Czechs don't like Jesuits. *Really* don't like them. Before the Thirty Years War, in 1618, the subjects living in the kingdom of Bohemia were divided about evenly between Catholic and Protestant. After the war the aristocratic protestants were driven into exile, mostly becoming known as the Moravian brethren, the rest being forced back into the Catholic Church. And it was the Jesuits who spearheaded the counter-reformation efforts, looking for heretics, burning prohibited books, such as the protestant edition of the Bible in the Czech language. Interesting; even the Bible can make it onto the Vatican Index of *Libri prohibiti*. Another surrealism, I suppose.

So, the Jesuits were not making mischief only in Bohemia. Here, their mission was to convert the Huron and baptize them. It ended after ten miserable years during which the numbers of Huron thinned as a result of smallpox and the number of missionaries was halved, eight of them ending their lives with an arrow through the rib cage. Today, the visitor finds a palisade protecting a few wooden houses, a black smithy, workshops, a chapel, small agricultural plots and a pier for canoes on the riverbank. An ordinary very small village. It doesn't match the image that lured us here. Which can happen easily when the imagination nourished by one continent is transplanted into another.

Looking around, and judging by today's standards, I have to conclude that the Jesuits didn't have an easy life here, though they could sleep under bear skins. Volunteering for a mission in which martyrdom was a distinct possibility called for certain kind of people, I guess. Other than that, the life was probably the same kind as life in a French village of the time, with the nearest neighbouring village just over the forest, just as in Europe, except the forest here stretched some thousand kilometres, all the way to Montreal. Thanks to that isolation, foreigners really could lose their lives at any moment. But the same thing could just as easily happen in France, and did, in the culminating religious war between Catholics and Hugenots.

In those days... we live in post-Einstein space-time continuum, so we have to imagine the France of those days not only as a different locale but within a different temporal frame as well. What was propelling the French villagers, A.D.1645 or so, to be at each others throats? I mean from the spiritual, mental and moral point of view? Well, nothing less was at stake than the salvation of the immortal soul. As soon as one realizes this fact, the relatively banal bucolic surroundings of the little tourist village at Lake Huron transform into backdrops for a drama of Shakespearean magnitude. On one side an uncompromisingly honest mission of the Jesuits to assure the souls of the natives their chance for salvation, on the other hand a desperate defence of personal and tribal identity expressed as faithfulness to their own spirituality, heritage, and the ways of their forefathers. Remind yourself that these were the days when Europe lived in the paradigm that postulated the soul as everyone's most precious possession.

Today, a big church commemorates the martyrs and their mission, and the reconstructed village is populated by students on summer jobs. The students play the Jesuits, clad in black robes, walking around, offering guidance, information and explanation. Since it seems that places connected with pushing any hard-line ideology are prone to inadvertent surrealist humour, I wasn't surprised at all when the black robe of one of the Jesuits opened to reveal a T shirt emblazoned with colourful royal flush and the words Las Vegas.

Alcatraz

I was quite satisfied with seeing Alcatraz from the outside and from a distance. I don't feel the need to enter a jail, touch the bars, look around, let my skin grow goose-bumps imagining what it was like inside, when it was buzzing with life and the air was thick with heavy curses and four-letter words were flying around. I don't need to listen to a retired prison guard telling me what famous criminal was behind these or those bars. For life. The ticket to this prison was one-way. Here, Sir, our jail was the all star jail, the most famous criminals of the USA were incarcerated behind those very bars, the cream of the crop, the champions in their field of endeavour... the speech of the guard would go something like this, because the notoriety would throw a flattering spotlight on him, too, a member of the elite, the cream of the crop of jail guards. Super-guard.

Don't such claims rub you the wrong way? Of course they do. That praise of criminals is a glorification of crime. How does a criminal become famous in the first place? Why should he? Why do those outcasts from decent society generate so much interest, if not sympathy, in the population at large? The media? Hollywood? Not themselves enough influence, I think. There must be something resonating deep in the human soul; otherwise Alcatraz wouldn't become a shrine of its kind. Perhaps there is a bit of identification with evil in the soul of even the most law-abiding citizen? Attraction to rebellion – and no matter against what? Anything, I guess, even the boredom of everyday work in a factory or a field. The seductive power of anarchy? Producing a sort of ambivalence: yes, he's a criminal, but there's something about him… Jesse James, Butch Cassidy, Billy the Kid, boot-hill graveyards. And fifty years later, though slightly differently Capone, Dillinger, Bonnie and Clyde.

I could somewhat understand the fascination with Wild West outlaws, history becoming folklore, blood and shattered bones washed and disinfected with the passing time. All the same, what is it that makes outlaws so attractive for an average American? Extreme individualism? Refusal to submit to authority? Any authority? Fascination with a strong personality? Misunderstood freedom? The lure of forbidden fruit? Do people come to visit Alcatraz acting on a mixture of those impulses combined with the need for seeing evidence of just rewards? After all, those bad guys met a bad end. But why are the historical criminals of the Wild West perceived as celebrities, almost heroes, the robbed banks and trains and dead bodies becoming just a sort of afterthought. Interesting times! The excitement of the rough Wild West! Yippee! Yes, we were a breed of toughies and we still are. Easy to romanticize, with a hundred years cushion, and with no danger that the six-shooters might start talking in the very same saloon where you're sipping your beer.

It's a stronger brew in the twentieth century. Al Capone or John Dillinger aren't such big heroes. The jury is still out on them, They are too close to us in time, not sanitized enough. They too closely resemble those types who today carry guns in the same streets you are walking and who might demand your wallet at any time. What brings a tourist to visit the Alcatraz in this case might be the need to see justice done, to enjoy the feeling that Al Capone suffered right here, right in front of your eyes, behind those very bars you're touching. Serves him right, the bastard. The Good guys won, the world is the way it should be. To feel such satisfaction, people are willing to pay cash and run aboard the little ship to take them to this spot of hell on earth. People are often interesting creatures. Anyway, I don't need to step on that island, even though, unlike the criminals who resided there, I could buy a return ticket.

Happy Destiny

Somewhere on the coast of California. A small city plaza. The sign above the store says: *Happy Destiny: palm-reading, tarots, crystal ball.* The shop window is dusty, the store empty except for some leaflets littering the dirty floor. There's an execution order on the door. He, or was it she, went bankrupt, closed up shop. Try his or her luck somewhere else. Idiot. A fortune teller couldn't tell his or her own future and lost a fortune. The cards lied. The seer didn't see. Bad advertising for her line of business. Maybe it wasn't a solid business anyway, didn't rest on solid foundations. Maybe she wasn't a very good fortune teller, hadn't learned her trade very well. As is often said, today's education isn't very good and doesn't prepare the student for life.

And then my reflection in the shop window glass shows me that the joke's on me. It transports me into the auditorium of the School of Economics in Prague. The professor did his utmost to plant in our minds how bad, how inferior to our socialist economy was the American system. Among the other arguments he threw at us was the number of yearly bankruptcies in America. We the students evaluated the information on the basis of what we knew, so we automatically considered the bankrupt enterprises to be big, and very big. In Czechoslovakia small business didn't exist at all, private business being strictly prohibited. When we heard *American business*, then we imagined General Electric, Chrysler, DuPont and the like. Maybe a bit smaller, but not much.

The professor failed to mention, so we didn't know, that a huge majority of American businesses were small businesses of the self-employed, family run, maybe with three or five employees. We didn't realize that, with so many bankruptcies, America would run out of businesses, it would have zero businesses, in a few years. We didn't know, we couldn't guess, how easy it was and is to start a business here, how many people would begin without having any idea how the laws of economics work and how to run a business. Before they manage to learn it, all that, of course, the business goes belly up. But the failure doesn't carry any particular stigma, the failures aren't cast out of society, aren't expelled from the lawn bowling club, don't lose their local library card. If they wish to, they simply open another business, maybe go bankrupt again, and if they are persistent, before their fifth or sixth attempt, all the failures have perhaps taught them how to manage a business, so that this time they succeed. In the meantime, they have provided statistical fodder for that bygone professor of mine. One has to spend a few years living here to figure out how things work and see through his lies.

What I would like to know now, considering this failed fortune-telling business, is whether the professor was misleading us because he didn't know any better and was just parroting what some other ignoramus had taught him, or he did know and lied to us deliberately. Ignorance isn't a sin? Really? For a teacher? For a teacher, ignorance in his field is a cardinal sin, because he's pushing into kid's heads a false representation of the world, giving them, so to speak, false coordinates of life. How are those poor souls supposed to make head or tail of such a world? Even without such misinformation there are plenty of places on the maps of life where lions roam and roar. If youngsters are misled by being mis-educated, is it any wonder that a number of them run into big problems later in life? They may go bankrupt not only in the business sense, having chosen to believe more in fortune-telling than in the laws of nature and rational thinking.

Beer in Pennsylvania

Dammit, I feel like a beer. So I thought when, in the falling dusk, we approached a campground in central Pennsylvania. We've travelled the whole day, having left New York City in the morning. In the camp office I noticed a Coke vending machine but none with beer. I asked the owner. She gave me a look as if I asked for a few grams of cocaine. Okay, no beer, I could do without beer. I'm not really a beer guy, I drink about a dozen beers a year, most of them on holidays.

The next day, we had a one-day vacation within our vacation. Vacation to the power of two. The day off after the thrills, and the expense, of New York. We spent the day in the pool. It was all ours, because there were very few other guests in that camp. Around four o'clock, the light afternoon breeze brought back my mind back to thinking about beer.

I left my family in the pool, started the van and drove away in search of the nearest gas station. In most parts of Canada you have to go to the Beer store to buy beer, but in the US you can get it in any store, at any gas bar. Properly cooled. But here I found neither cold beer nor any other beer at the gas station. Strange, but maybe the guy working there was in AA and didn't want to be tempted. I kept driving. I would find my beer, no problem. I was in the US. A General store at the next intersection carried no beer either. And I got a look as if I had said something obscene. Was beer a swear word around here? It is a four letter word, after all. I kept driving, accumulating almost twenty five kilometres and failing at another gas station and a corner store. How come? The growing confusion mutated into growing determination. Now I really did want that beer and I would get it no matter what.

In the bar of a small local hotel, the barman told me that he would be pleased to sell me a glass of draft but I would have to drink it inside the bar. He couldn't sell me a bottle or a can, even if he had one, not even if I offered him a golden calf for it. My face must have been very legible. Barmen are usually savvy people and talkative, too, so I finally learned from him that there are all kinds of states in the US, and that Pennsylvania is inhabited by a large number of religious groups, some of them fundamentalist, who voted for consigning the sale of any alcoholic beverage to a few specialized stores. The Great Battle against the sin of alcoholism, you understand. I did. In his turn, he understood my need to commit a minor sin on holidays and explained to me, sketching the route on a napkin, how to get into town and find a Beer barn. It's not too far, he said, about fifteen miles. In the meantime, I could buy a cold one from him. No, thank you, I replied, I never drink when I drive. Nobody would care around here, not even the cops. No, not really, that's my law.

Another fifteen miles is not exactly close, but buying the beer became a matter of prestige. I found the city. I found the Beer barn. One can of beer? Ha ha, we don't sell singles. Six pack? No six-packs either. Get serious, man. A dozen? I said, get serious. The only size you can get is twenty four.

Only two hours after I had left, I re-entered the swimming pool. I had my beer in my hand. I enjoyed it. Not only was it good, but the taste was enhanced by the hardship of getting it. I drank another one at the campfire in the evening. The question is – when am I going to drink the remaining twenty two? Well, the good intentions of law-givers very often pave the way to hell... battle with alcoholism, eh... I wanted just a single beer.

Terra sacra

California isn't a bad name but this stretch of land could easily be called something else. The word California describes something like a fictitious paradise, something from the relations of El Dorado, and Shangri La. Well, it does have the reputation of being an earthly paradise, doesn't it, even though, only two hundred miles from the paradisal coast, Death valley spreads, and only a few places on Earth, with the possible exception of Hawaiian volcanoes, are as close to Hell as is this desert. But close encounters of paradise and hell are quite frequent on earth, so we don't need to dwell on them.

To tell the truth, I feel like this part of America should carry a name like Saintsland, Sacraland, or something along those lines, because even a glance at local names on the map tells you that a huge number of Saints have their domicile here. Many more than in the whole Bible belt. I had no idea that there were so many saints. From Santa Agatha to San Zeno. Of course, the Spaniards who colonized the land are the real aficionados when it comes to the saints, and Mexicans are no slouches in this department either. Beside the names of major saints, like the Apostles, that everybody knows, you can find here the names of Saints that you probably didn't know existed, like San Quentin of the notorious prison. Did you know that Quentin was a Saint's name? How about San Ardo? Santa Venetia?

Speaking of the names, I wonder how naming worked in the early days of settling this land. I imagine that everybody wanted for their little fields and cluster of houses a major saint, somebody close to the Lord's throne, somebody with influence. There are not enough major saints to satisfy the demand and, since the Catholics like a hierarchy, there must be a pecking order. So, how come, we don't here encounter a dozen settlements named after Peter and Paul and Andrew and Luke? Did somebody coordinate the naming? Judge the conflicts? Did they have street brawls over the names? Why do you find San Rafael here, wasn't he one of the archangels? Was he demoted to mere sainthood? I wonder, too, what ecclesiastical authority approved the name San Bernardino – not Bernard but Bernardino, a diminutive. The same goes for San Benito. To diminish a saint is quite an achievement.

What kind of psychological set up did this naming reflect? What impact did it have? To invoke a saint in the local name means requesting heavenly protection of that place. Compare this with the rest of America, full of places called Fort This and Fort That. You either ask for protection or protect yourself, be passive or active. Maybe this propensity for relying on the influence of saints was the reason why the Spaniards lost the Southwest. Unlike California, the rest of America was *pursuing* happiness, not passively asking for it.

And who, in his right mind, could come up with the idea of naming a city *El Pueblo de Nuestra Senora la Reina de Los Angelos del Rio Porciunculo*. No wonder somebody shortened it first to Los Angeles – leaving out the main person, the Queen of Heaven – and then to L.A. This must be the world record for shortening a local name. I understand. I wouldn't like to be, say, a telegraph operator with Union Pacific, having to transmit the full city name with every dispatch. Or try writing a poem or a song to celebrate a city with such a name. Is it any wonder that the capital of this conclave of saints is called Sacramento? Might not the name of Saintsland or, simply, Heaven, be more fitting?

Maybe not. I find it interesting that all those patron saints, supposed to keep a protective eye over the population, somehow lost control. Just imagine meek and humble San Francis spending a few weeks in the city dedicated to him, named after him, the city he represents as an ambassador in Heaven. California's lifestyle, especially her laws don't exactly seem to be shining examples of Christian piety and virtues. I don't know; not being a theologian, I tiptoe away from the subject. I will just add that the California might be the right name, after all.

Boot Hills

"What am I going to do about you, you rascal, you're going to end up in Boot-Hill". So many a mother all over the West lamented at about the time when Iron Horses started to displace the buffaloes, just as their Czech counterparts expressed the same worries by shouting at their unruly off-spring: "You're growing up for jail."

Boot Hill graveyard is an effective expression because it's a metaphor. It doesn't really need any explanation. The graveyard of those who left this world with their boots on. Will they be wearing them at the Last Judgement, among all the barefoot others? Never mind. In short, Boot Hill is a graveyard for those whose demise was quick and violent, mostly arranged by the products of Messrs. Smith & Wesson, Colt and Winchester. The slow ones in the saying, "the quick and the dead". Honourable and respected citizens were passing to the Eternity in their beds, under comforters, surrounded by their family and barefoot. Dying with your boots on must have been a lose-lose situation. Your fellow gunslingers looked down their noses at you because you were not quick enough; the burghers of Abilene or Deadwood or Tombstone saw you as outcast, hell-riser, rascal, troublemaker and general nuisance, to be avoided at any cost. Meeting you on the street spelled trouble for them, getting beaten and robbed at best, being humiliated by gunfire at the feet in a worse case, and taking some lead between the eyes or the ribs in the case of those born under unfavourable stars.

Boots on the feet of a corpse meant a serious stigma, marking outsiders even after their death, placing them for ever in the quarantine of a separate graveyard, reflecting the deep abyss between God-fearing, law-abiding citizens and those who didn't take God or the law seriously enough. I can vividly imagine the nightmares some citizens must have had, haunted by the idea that they might suffer a heart attack on the street and die on the spot, o terror, with their boots on... the gossip! The shame! Such a passing could blemish a whole impeccable life as hunter, gold prospector, and highly esteemed proprietor of the best whorehouse in town. To die with the boots on meant a disorderly death, with no confession, no last rites, a death somehow against nature.

Today the expression is just an antiquated metaphor. Maybe we have become more tolerant of rascals and their evils. We don't insist – literally beyond the grave – on demanding adherence to mainstream virtues. Besides, we seldom have time to notice how somebody died. Many more people die with their boots on, in our days. Nowadays the biggest killers aren't the lightning-fast heirs of Billy the Kid. By no means, the diseases of our civilization, like heart attack or stroke can draw so fast that you don't even see the blasting gun, much less manage to get your boots off.

Well, these days Boot Hills are a minor local tourist attraction, frequented by relatively few visitors. In the Happy Hunting Grounds of language, the idiom is a document of the poetic sense of our forefathers.

Monte Vegas

Gambling is synonymous with Monte Carlo. Green roulette tables surrounded by gentlemen in tuxedos and slick hair, ladies with gowns cut so low that you never notice their diamond earrings. The conversation is quiet, sophisticated, a bit decadent. Champagne waits in silver ice buckets, cut crystal glasses reflect flashes of light. In short, the casino is frequented by so-called better people. At least in Europe, at least according to books and movies.

Cut.

The large glass door slides open and from the humidity of the midnight city (why such humidity when the city lies in the desert?) we enter into an air-conditioned space the size of two hockey arenas. A moving sea of bobbing human heads and faces. A man in a checkered shirt and an inspector-Clouseau-style hat is walking towards us, leading a lady who looks like an overstuffed down pillow and who should have discarded those pink shorts twenty years and fifty kilograms ago. For Christ's sake! Isn't this a casino? Baseball hats, T-shirts of all colours and stages of cleanliness, with and without prints, just two ties in sight and one bow tie, unfortunately on a checkered flannel shirt, running shoes and sandals. Oh my! Where is the haute couture, the shining shoes, the low cut gowns and pearl necklaces? Where did all the style go? Well, here we are in Las

Vegas and Las Vegas is in America and, in accordance with the US constitution, Las Vegas gives everybody a chance to lose their money, without discrimination on any basis.

Las Vegas is a city spread in a desert. As Wikipedia informs, Las Vegas always had a tolerance for adult forms of entertainment. Well, sure, this makes sense, there being no other way to lure people into a desert than turning a blind eye to what is considered vice anywhere else. Even the fundamentalist puritans in the surrounding states can tolerate such an accommodating attitude, believing that the desert will protect them. Besides, they wisely realize that it is good policy to provide some outlet for people who have to gamble no matter what. If you have to, you have to; go to Las Vegas and don't expose *our* community to temptation. We're quite satisfied with an occasional poker game behind closed doors and drawn curtains. After all, a temporary, short-term easing up of morals used to be official at all times and all around the world – permission to run wild and have a great time once a year - carnivals, Mardi Gras, feasts, bacchanalia... you know what I mean. The uniqueness of Las Vegas and its claim to fame consists of stretching those few days into the whole year. Vice and sin are so common place here that they can't be seen as a holiday activities, so there's no reason to get excited about anything so banal, look forward to it, dress up for it. The exception is the rule here. What dialectically follows, or should, is that once a year local folks celebrate a feast of anti-bacchanalia, behaving for a few days so piously impeccable, that the following confession would bore even the soul of the most desiccated priest to death.

In front of the long rows of one-armed bandits are sitting those who have accepted their flashing challenge to duel. It is like the finale of western movies – one on one. With a plastic pail of ammunition handy, hundreds of coins, they shoot round after round after round. But the one-armed bandit has many lives; as if it stepped out of a computer game, it can absorb an unbelievable amount of bullets before one hits the right spot that forces him to cough up some of your coin. I don't know how exciting it is for the player, because the expressions on their faces are rather blank, sort of no-expression, fuzzy, absent, spiritless. The one-armed bandit, hectic flashing notwithstanding, doesn't appear excited either. He has seen, faced and survived crowds of opponents like this. After all, he runs the whole show; you just finance it and push the buttons. Any skills you might have are irrelevant.

Maybe this is why the players' eyes have a peculiar expression. Though wide open, they are immovable, staring at the bandit like into a snake's eyes. Their fingers feed the slots with nickles and dimes without feeling the coins, their arms crank the bandit's arm without the brain being aware of giving the order to do so. Anything requiring thought seems to be irrelevant, if not detrimental here. Within a few minutes of playing, a soul-endowed human being is transformed into a robot, the Descartesian mechanism, the system of levers, pulleys, wheel and axles, inclined planes. She's duelling another system of levers, wheel and axles and planes, robot against robot. If such a player had to pull the same lever for a whole day at work, let's say minting coins, he or she would consider that boring, even degrading, while here she delights in voluntarily giving up her coins, throwing them into the bandit's bottomless pocket. On second thought, all those machines appear to be a long row of small altars to Mammon, altars for worshippers who bring sacrifices in the form of dimes and quarters, mumbling a short prayer – make me rich! Somehow, they forget that Mammon has no interest in making them rich. All Mammon wants is to keep getting richer himself; at best he wants you to worship his riches.

A little bit to the side, a number of semicircular tables hosts card games. Black jack, poker. Mostly men play around here, and with a variety of expressions on their faces. Here you can see wrinkled foreheads, eyes x-raying an opponent, fingers scratching the chin, hair standing on end, rivulets of sweat disappearing under a collar, the tapping of a shoe. Maybe because in this case skills play a role, the player is an active participant who can influence the outcome, to some degree it's in his own hands whether he leaves with a wad of dollars in the back pocket of his pants or without any pants at all. By the way, I haven't seen anybody without pants. Maybe the pantless are shoved out discreetly.

And here we are – here she is, Queen of all casinos, roulette. The green table is not even half the size of those you see in the movies. Two or three players sit around it; the rest of the chairs are empty. Behind the chairs people are walking, whistling, talking, running... this place has all the cosiness of a railway station platform. It's impossible to generate any feeling of the excitement of high end gambling. It's like playing craps on a sidewalk, like a drive-through wedding and a drive-through wedding reception, with the wedding night somewhere out in the back alley. If, by some chance, a lady in a low cut gown, with a diamond necklace, were to come and sit at this table, the croupier would probably forget to toss the ball in the roulette. Really, the whole Atlantic ocean separates the world of roulette here and in Monte Carlo. Maybe this kind of depravity doesn't emigrate well. This society is too young and dynamic to cultivate decadence as an art form. Unless all this is for plebs, and somewhere else, behind the door that a thousand dollar bill opens... who knows.

As you stroll through this gambling den, you realize suddenly that there is not a single chair, no love seat, no bench, settee or indeed anything to sit on. You can sit only when you play. It's a pity, because right here, behind a corner, attracted by the music, you find a very good band backing an excellent soul singer. You could enjoy listening to them, if you could just sit down for a while. You could use a bit of spirit in this den of spiritual emptiness.

The High After Noon

I didn't see my first Western movie until I was thirteen. It was called *High Noon*. True, it was whispered that comrade Stalin loved Westerns and could watch them by the dozen, but he must have concluded that those fairy tales of good and evil for grown-ups, might inspire undesirable yearnings in his subjects. So, I had to wait till my thirteenth year. The movie was a big hit; people waited in long lines to see it. We kids were thrilled, though one of my teachers, tongue in cheek, put it down saying that the movie isn't very generous. For four crowns admission we see only four bad guys gunned down, which makes it one guy for one crown, while in the westerns of his youth you could get a bad guy dead for a quarter, even a dime. We had to wait a couple more years to enjoy a similar ratio, till the time when the Magnificent Seven, guns blazing, made their way to our silver screens. And that's just about all I can recall concerning westerns. John Wayne was undesirable because he was a conservative, Clint Eastwood for unknown reasons. Towards the end of the seventies, Dustin Hoffman made an appearance as Little Big man and that was about it.

Sure, on Canadian television we could watch Westerns, which we called 'horses asses tales', usually around midnight, but I managed to more or less ignore them. They seemed almost boring. Everything calls for the right age and mental stage, I guess, and Westerns came too late for me. Westerns are in essence fairy-tales, despite the fact that in them unshaven actors with dirt under their fingernails are pretending tooth and nail to be real characters living real lives. A more mature person knows very well from experience that the victory of good over evil is by no means a straightforward business, and that the punishment for evil-doing can be long in coming, or inadequate, or even completely absent. Such a person is a sceptic; sensing that those stories are overstuffed with the fantasy, he isn't as able to identify with the plot, action and catharsis as readily as a relatively naive green mind in its salad years.

Then, one summer day, driving from Deadwood in the Black hills of South Dakota to the Devil's tower, we could see about fifty head – as the English language has it – of cattle crossing the road. The herd was being driven by three men on horses. Checkered shirts, stetsons, lassos on the saddle horn, colts on the hip – oh my, I thought, are those guys really real cowboys? Looking at them I realized that being a cowboy was, at least in Czechoslovakia, synonymous with adventure. A cowboy was a professional horse-riding adventurer. A similarly misleading image is projected by today's rodeo – in this case the image of a pro athlete. It seems that, under the influence of movies and books, myth totally displaced reality, completely obscuring the fact that being a cowboy is a job, and not an easy one. It calls not only for being a virtuoso on a horse or with a lasso, but also in forking manure. There are other jobs like this, like pirate. Mythologizing this job dropped scrubbing the deck on your knees with a deck-brush, endless climbing up and down rope ladders, boredom in the crow's-nest while it rains.

And then you run into the reality and it wakes you up and you see that the whole cowboy myth has been, soberly speaking, about employment in the livestock industry with the possible sub-category of transportation, if you consider cattle drives from Texas to the railway in the North.

Pity. Another adventure zone up in smoke, proving itself to be a myth. One more illusion lost; we are a little bit older again.

Weekend in Fredonia

Returning from the North rim of the Grand Canyon, you see the motel of the same name as soon as you enter Fredonia. The motel consists of two parts; one is an ordinary row of contemporary motel rooms, the other, a hundred meters up the road, is a different cup of tea, a more than hundred fifty years old two storey wooden structure, a hotel since the earliest days of local settlement, back in the days when the action depicted today in westerns, so often filmed in the vicinity of this town, was the reality of everyday life. In those days, the ten guest-rooms most likely housed travelling salesmen with firearms, or whiskey, a few card sharks, some prospectors, and maybe, occasionally, a real-estate man. There's a beautifully carved wooden gun cabinet in the former kitchen, capable of holding quite a few guns. We are assigned a suite in this hotel, probably because the elderly Mormon couple in reception concluded that my wife and I shouldn't share a room with our adult son.

When I tried to drive from the reception to the hotel, I couldn't. The starter didn't work. We'll have a look at it tomorrow, the old guy at reception says.

I tell you, the best place to watch the original Zorro, the black and white movie with Douglas Fairbanks, is in this ancient hotel. It could be a prop in the movie. So could the surrounding red Arizona semi-desert and the silence. Of course, the movie is silent, too.

The next morning is Saturday, of course - all automotive break-downs happen just before or on the weekend. The local car shop is closed, Judd having gone to the wedding of one of his nieces. We inspect the problem with the old man but can't put our fingers on it. "Well, you can stay here till Monday", he says, "we'll take a good care of you". He looks imperturbable, like nothing could ever throw him off balance. He's lived all his life around here, in the vicinity of the Grand Canyon. It seems like he has been soaked in the Canyon's timelessness. In daylight he does look old, younger than the Grand Canyon, sure, by not by much. I share with him the fact that starting from here on Monday will give us only six days to make it home, across half the continent, before our vacation is over. "What's the hustle, why rush anywhere?" the oldie says. "Slow down, enjoy your weekend here, relax. You eastern people, are always running somewhere, as if you forgot how to walk, let alone stand still. You're dashing somewhere all the time, hurrying, hassling, your eyes focused on something in the future, so sooner or later you overlook a heart attack or a stroke or something else in your way and stumble over it. For once, enjoy the western tempo of living, indulge the feeling that there's nothing you can do.

Soccer final

The ground floor of our hotel boasts a parlour furnished with older but 'better pieces'. It projects an atmosphere of class with a touch of the Wild West. The biggest piece is a huge, richly carved mahogany secretaire with lots of small drawers and a tilted desk, in case some guest needs to compose a long letter. Even a glass inkwell is provided, though it contains no ink. On the opposite wall an upright piano invites guests with its slightly honky-tonk tuning. Hearing it immediately conjures an image of a smoke-filled saloon, with a long row of cowboys leaning against the bar and ogling the high kicking legs of can-can dancers on the stage. Above the piano a huge realistic painting depicting a grazing buffalo herd gives the room an artistic touch. The middle of the room is occupied by a huge couch and two armchairs arranged in semi-circle around a console TV set. Here we make ourselves comfortable to watch the final match of the World Soccer Championship – the Superbowl of the soccer world, played once every four years. We're looking forward to it, since Brazil, our favourite team, is one of the sides. We're waiting for couple more people to come. The old guy told us about them. They are not guests, but people just passing through town but don't want to miss the game. Why not – more people should mean more fun.

Two travellers. A young, intelligent looking man and his fiancée. French nationals. Ah yes, that makes sense, France being the other contestant in the final. The young man is a recently graduated architect who has just completed a year of post-graduate studies at Columbia university. He invited his fiancée for a vacation tour of the US and they just have made it to Fredonia. The man speaks good English so we can talk a bit.

We, the three men, are sitting on the couch facing the screen. Our ladies, not really interested in soccer, sit in armchairs in the wings. The teams are on the green field. When the first bars of the Marseillaise are played, I feel the architect stiffen for a moment, as if he wants to jump up and stand in attention, but then he realizes that he doesn't have to, not being in the Paris stadium but in red Arizona desert. So he just straightens up his backbone, juts his chin forward and hums in a low voice: *"Allons enfants de la Patrie..."* Not being familiar with the Brazilian anthem, we can't reciprocate in style.

A whistle, and here we go. In ten minutes, the architect moves from his relaxed position forward to sit on the very edge of the couch. Then he starts driving his nails into the wood of the coffee table in front of him. His breathing is growing faster, his eyes are taking on an odd sheen. *Putain!* he barks suddenly after a foul is called and the ensuing free kick means a danger for his goal. The following torrent of rapid French contains several more *putains*. Strange, there's no player of this name on the field. From now on, he's shouting more and more often and I notice that he associates most of the players with *putain*. A nickname? A position on the team? My once relatively decent French, acquired many years ago at school, has been eradicated by the passage of thirty years since graduation and fifteen years of living in anglophone Canada. Now I would not be able to buy a newspaper or a baguette in France or Québec. And then, somehow, I realized that *putain* means whore. Don't ask why I remembered this word, guaranteed not to be acquired in the classroom and never used in my life. Maybe I learned it from some good book.

Goal! Shit. The French score. Monsieur ejects himself from the couch, arms reaching for the ceiling, runs around the room, pummelling the wall with his fists, shouting alternately *Goal!* and *Vive la France!* God forbid that Brazilians should score the equalizer now. He'd suffer a heart attack and our show would be over. Or we'd have to jump out the window. This is the kind of the fan who's ready to kill for his team. And after all, we are in the Wild West.

Since that goal, he hasn't sat much. Every *putain* has been synchronized with leaping up and every leap accompanied with *putain*. Each and every player has been *putain* at least five times over. If he were cursing the Brazilians, I could understand, but his own team? Well, a different country, a different way of rooting for his boys. I mean *putains*. His fiancée looks indifferent, even a bit bored, so his way of cheering must be quite ordinary. Maybe she's contemplating her future marriage with this guy.

He's left the couch for most of the second half. His eyes shine with real insanity now, his voice is becoming raspy and hoarse. For the last ten minutes of the game, bitter for my son and me, he kneels in front of the couch mumbling a mixture of prayers and *putains*. The final whistle. For the last time he

springs up, runs around the couch five times, with his arms above his head as if he has personally scored all three goals, dances, hugs the chair in which his fiance is still sitting. The Buffalo in the painting interrupted their grazing long ago and are watching him, loudly mooing their confusion. Accepting our congratulations for the victory of his side, he runs outside, into the street, shouting at the top of his voice, for the whole of Fredonia, for the whole of Arizona to hear: *Champions du Monde! Vive la France!* Yet, this doesn't seem celebration enough for him, so he bursts back inside, tears off the piano keyboard lid, attacks the ivories and tries to flutter and thunder with the remnants of his voice:
Allons enfants de la Patrie
Le jour de gloire est arrivé...

We take French leave.

We sit on the front porch for a long while occasionally watching a slowly drifting little cloud. We sit on the back porch spending half an hour observing a three inch long beetle. We listen to coyotes' howling at dusk. Little by little, we relax – we really can't do anything else. It might be the Grand Canyon's influence. As the sights of it and into it percolate through our minds, we realize that there are other than human scales, bigger, timeless, endless as the Universe itself - divine, if you wish. When you stand on the rim of the Canyon, you automatically whisper, without really realizing it. That's the way it should be. You *are* tiny. Insignificant. That light of timelessness shows the relative frivolity of most hectic of the human activities, chaotic pursuits, nervousness, stress for this or that reason. The Grand Canyon really couldn't care less about your becoming office head after ten years of manoeuvring and scheming, about who won the soccer championship, about approaching or departing economic depression. Those rocks completely ignore all the upheavals and conflicts rocking our society. They are absolutely indifferent as to whether these politics or that politician is better than the other. They have ignored it all, all the big shots, from the Egyptian deities after whom lots of features here are named, to the crowds of kings and chiefs and imperators to the chairmen and presidents to the heads that are crowned, mitred, feathered, or simply bigger than average. They all vanished in the blink of an eye. Only the Canyon lasts. And lasts, offering its visitors the view *sub specie aeternitatis*. Even though we human beings don't have eternity at our disposal, it never hurts to look inside ourselves, now and then from this angle.

Whistler

A marvellous mountain they have here, two of them at that, really marvellous. One of the most famous ski resorts in North America. In the same league as Vail or Aspen. Must offer wonderful skiing. Around the summit, there is even a big piece of glacier so you can ski in summer too. Like today, mid-July, you may meet a person in T-shirt and sandals but with skis on his shoulder or a snowboard under her arm. We are tempted to take a lift to the summit to enjoy the wonderful view of surrounding rocky peaks, but even in summer, off season, the tickets for three of us would cost way over a hundred bucks. You know what you can do with your views, then. The town looks good, though perhaps a little too big for a ski resort – in winter it would require lots of walking in ski boots just to get to the lifts, even taking a city bus. Only the most expensive hotels have a ski-in, ski-out location.

The ambiance... how to put it without being offensive... seems to be a bit too self-conscious. People, younger or older, seem to take great care to look right, to wear the right designer sunglasses, to show off the right designer T-shirts and shorts, following this or that idiot who momentarily arbitrates what's cool and what's not. When the snobbery hangs in the air like humidity even now, I don't want to see it in winter, let alone after the Olympics. The games are going to elevate this good resort into a super playground for super snobs. I can imagine a winter promenade of ladies bristling with real furs and gentlemen in five thousand dollars snow-suits, carrying the most expensive skis over their shoulders.

Well, let's go to McDonald's, which should be as good as anywhere else. Not quite. They don't have the strawberry sundae I wanted and we can't get some other things either. So be it, let's say there are way too many tourists here in the summer. Leaving McDonald's, I discover in the parking lot that somebody has made a yellow chalk mark on the tire of my car. Presumably it's because the posted sign asserts that parking for more than an hour is prohibited here and some attendant wanted to mark our arrival. Mind you, it's not paid parking. It's nobody's business how long I shop here. Isn't Whistler in Canada? OK, relax guys, I am gone, won't stay a minute longer.

And yet, looking into the rear-view mirror, I have to whisper wistfully – those two mountains... they look so wonderful...

Singer Heritage

Even minor league inventors, those who became famous for other things than inventing, could make, not millions but tens of millions. One such inventor was Mr. Singer. Yes, I mean Mr. Sewing Machine himself. His machines were well known in Czechoslovakia, though not the recent and latest productions. The foot-propelled ones, manufactured well before World War II and even the Great War. Fifty, seventy, even a hundred year old machines, passed from grandma to Ma to daughter, enjoyed a great reputation, being considered superior to contemporary products, let's say of Ruritanian origin, that were sold in stores. Nothing can handle six-time-folded denim better than a Singer, young initiates of sewing confided to each other. This whole world-wide empire rested on a simple invention, the crucial idea of placing the eye of the needle in the point of the needle. But I don't want to talk about that.

While roaming New England, we followed the Mohawk Trail along the northern border of Massachusetts. Driving through the town of Williamstown we saw a sign for the Clark Institute of Art. Well, it's exceedingly easy to get me to visit an art gallery. I could be dragged there on a cooked noodle, as the Czech idiom goes. The grandfather of Mr. Clark, the collector, was a director of the Singer Sewing company and the collection was paid for with inherited money. I wondered if it might contain a painting of a Parisian midinette – popular term used in the day of Impressionists for a Parisian seamstress - leaning over a Singer... never mind.

For two hours we feasted mostly on impressionist and post-impressionist beauty. Most impressive, though not a top collection, not compared to some others. Mostly unfamiliar paintings of the very familiar, great names. Walking through that large museum building, I realized that America is a different world indeed, very different from what I imagined, from what I expected. In Czechoslovakia in my day, you might inherit an ancient sewing machine; here is evidence of a fortune huge enough to pay for an extremely expensive collection. It is mind-boggling, to my mind at least, that a person could own this Monet, could have it in his home, you understand, his *home*. To display *Two piano playing girls* by Renoir above the fireplace in his living room... pray at home at the original Gothic altar painted in 1354, or view a Modigliani nude on the wall of his bedroom. The impression one had in Czechoslovakia was that such paintings, such names, could be found only in museums, that only museums have enough money to buy them. True, sometimes in an art book you would find a note saying: Rockefeller or Mellon or Guggenheim collection, but those names sounded somewhat impersonal, rather institutional. They were so much larger-than-life that they couldn't belong to real living people. Those collections were perceived as a private museum, so to speak. On second thought, those people must have more money than most museums. I wonder if they like their paintings. Never mind again.

In here, a descendant of a director of Singer company had over hundred paintings. I'd better get used to the idea that the gentlemen who were successful here were making really big money, of a magnitude unimaginable in Czechoslovakia, and that buying a Cezanne for your dining room or a Renoir for your wife's boudoir is a prerequisite of success. Maybe even part and parcel of success. Who knows, maybe for such people to buy an original was equivalent to me buying a good reproduction.

Another line of thinking flows from the stroll through this museum – how many pictures did those famous guys paint? One is familiar with maybe twenty, maybe forty of their paintings from reproductions, but that must be just the tip of the iceberg when just one collector like Mr. Clark, neither the biggest nor the most famous of the connoisseurs, can amass well over a hundred. How many paintings are hanging on the walls of other collectors or even non-collectors? How many canvases repose in bank vaults, owned by people who never have to look at them because they would see just dollars signs anyway? Never mind for the third time. Isn't it a pity that of the thousands of paintings of this or that painter, we can know only a dozen or so? Well, I'm glad that I could see this hundred.

Birch Canoe

In adventure books about Canada, a canoe was mentioned now and then. Not often enough to do justice to the role of the canoe in the Canadian history, I can see now. The main means of transportation for literary adventurers were legs, horses or, farther North, dogsled teams. The omission of the canoe betrays a huge authorial ignorance. Without the canoe, Canada wouldn't be what she is. For two hundred years Canadian history revolved around the canoe, floated on the canoe, and, without it, would have sunk.

When the French established Quebec city in 1608 and started to settle along the St. Lawrence River, their explorers were called *courriers du bois* or forest runners. I don't think they could do much forest running, since they must have had a really hard time squeezing through something that was unknown in most of Europe of that time – an impenetrable primeval bush. They couldn't have penetrated very far. So they quickly learned from the Indians the art of building birch bark canoes. Only then could Canada as we know it get her start. Over the following hundred years, the French developed a regular canoe connection via Ottawa river, Lake Huron, Lake Superior and the Mississippi river with New Orleans, their other possession in America. Long distance paddling. That's why here and there they established rest areas and refreshment points – places with French names like Saint Louis,

Dubuque, Detroit. Then the French lost their battle with the British and were left with Quebec only.

In Canada, the British were coming at them from the flank, from the North. When king Charles II established the Hudson Bay company in 1670, he endowed it with all the lands draining into Hudson Bay. Poor chap, he had no idea, how generous he was being. What a time to be on the receiving side of Royal largesse! Would he have given such gift if he really knew the size of it? With His Royal signature he transferred into private hands about half of today's Canada and a bit of the US as well. Consequently, the HBC started to penetrate the continent from Hudson Bay, while their competitors, the North West company, charged West from Montreal. For the following two hundred years, most cargo transportation in Canada used the canoe. Canada had a topography very suitable for water travel. It is said that it is possible to paddle a canoe from the Atlantic ocean to both the Pacific and Arctic oceans via waterways, and that the longest portage would still be less than 20 kilometres. It was a Northwest passage of sorts, but for retail business only, so it didn't count with the big shots in London.

I have to wonder what kind of tough guys were living in Canada back then. Just imagine, having to paddle for three months, seven days a week, to paddle your way upstream with a fully loaded canoe from Montreal to somewhere beyond lake Winnipeg, and then make it back in another ninety days. Gracious heavens! That is a journey about as long as a crusade to the Holy land! About equally adventurous and dangerous. How come no troubadour or poet has immortalized such a journey in an epic poem? Such an expedition is an odyssey, an undertaking rivalling the campaign of Charlemagne into Spain, or the quest for the Holy Grail. How is it, then, that an arm with a sword has been celebrated in songs and poems, while an arm with a paddle has been ignored and overlooked? Either there was no Canadian poet of sufficient ability around back then or he was refused passage aboard – space and weight must have been at premium.

I think that, regardless of heraldic rules, a canoe and an arm armed with a paddle should be a part of the Canadian Coat of Arms. Even in the case of the big discovery voyages of Mackenzie and Fraser the canoe isn't mentioned as a prominent factor of their success. And there is a general ignorance about the speed record of HBC governor Sir George Simpson. His executive birch canoe, with twelve Metis paddlers, covered the distance from Hudson bay to Vancouver – circa 5000 kilometres – in an unbelievable 65 days. I'd like to see today's Olympians on the same route. And how about this - CEOs can command for themselves anything from limos to jets, but an express canoe as a movable CEO office, that's something unheard of in today's world of Big Business - without a secretary, too, all the eligible ladies having refused because of mosquitoes.

Since those days water transportation has modernized and motorized, of course, but the canoe remains as a vessel of fun and sport. With a pedigree like that, canoeing was destined to become a Canadian ritual. Though it is not included in the official requirements for citizenship, canoeing belongs there unofficially, together with tasting of maple sirup, witnessing an NHL game, chopping down a tree using the beaver system and being interviewed by Peter Gzowski.

For all those reasons, plus curiosity, we rented a canoe while camping in the Algonquin park. We got the canoe on the water of Tea lake without major mishap, though we registered that it is very touch and go when it comes to lateral stability. The water was still as a mirror. Within ten minutes, all three of us managed to get inside without leaving any paddle ashore. Without getting wet. In an hour, or so it seemed, of exceedingly careful, almost breathless, paddling in a zigzag manner we covered about three hundred metres and reached a small uninhabited island. Disembarking was a bit faster than embarking. Lie on your back, breath deeply, enjoy your rest. Rest mainly mental. We found wild mushrooms, very good ones, plenty of them. On the way back we breathed a bit more often and made it ten minutes faster. Practice makes... let's say better. At this speed we could reach Winnipeg in about twenty years. To keep the experience historical, we had the dinner from local sources – the fried mushrooms. Maybe we could have survived around here even back then, but I would definitely prefer not to paddle for the HBC or its governor.

Big Canoe

How would you like to experience near sea-sickness without being really sick? Drive or walk aboard the big ferry called Chi Cheemaun, or, in the language of the pale faces, Big Canoe. It will take you from Tobermory at the tip of the Bruce peninsula to Manitoulin island. All on Lake Huron.

Through its high lifted bow, the ferry swallows a full parking lot of cars, trucks and RVs. Then a sailor on the front deck leaves his high-tech control panel, grabs a broom and strikes the metal deck with its handle three times. Why he doesn't use his walkie-talkie, I don't know. Some old custom of striking the rhythm for the oarsmen, surviving from Viking times? Upon this signal, the bow begins to descend, the engines start to churn the water and you're on your way.

You're sailing for an hour, an hour and a half, the lake is calm and yet a feeling of the lightest discomfort starts creeping in the vicinity of your stomach, as if it were lightened, negligibly, just by a force equal to the weight of the liquid displaced by your stomach. At first you can't guess what the sensation might be, then you start to suspect the onset of sea-sickness. But we are on a lake! Lake-sickness? There's no such thing. Still, it's weird – the ship is massive, doesn't really rock, the lake is calm and is not a sea.

Not a sea – but very close. In our early days in Canada, before I could really see the lakes, I used to be very surprised each time I heard or read about some wreck lifted from the lake bottom, or about a ship sinking in a storm, in 1846, say. Or even throughout the twentieth century. Nonsense, ships don't wreck on a lake. Not the big ship. That's what your European thinking tells you because it lacks experience with a lake you can't see across. Great lakes are unimaginable in the scale of Europe. Each of them is bigger than some European nations. They are huge, veritable fresh water seas. They even have noticeable tides.

About shipwrecking... the Lakes used to be quite busy, and not only with canoe traffic, since early in the nineteenth century three-masted tall ships were sailing the waters as well. The city of Port Burwell on Lake Erie was famous for shipbuilding because of the dense forest of quality wood in its vicinity. And I don't mean scaled down ships; no. They built full size vessels, capable of sailing the Atlantic. Gales and storms on the lakes were no laughing matter, wind can easily tear away the sails, break the mast, a wave or two floods the deck, and down goes the ship. The result might even be a Crusoe or two, the shores being so wild and unpopulated.

Well, talking about all that has made you forget about your stomach and now you are crossing only a lake, after all. We're already dropping the anchor at the Manitoulin Island, so you have almost experienced sea-sickness but weren't really sick. Just as I promised.

Manitou's Backyard

The name Manitou was a household name in Czechoslovakia. No wonder, because every boy met him during his reading adventures, and every father used to be a boy. Like so many other things, seen from Bohemia, Manitou was just an idea. In the adventure books he figured only as a name. As a deity, he didn't seem to be demanding. Though the Creator of everything and everybody, he didn't demand the erection of temples, or even of altars, didn't require religious services and didn't require any priesthood. He didn't ask even for a prayer. He himself controlled both the our World and the Netherworld known as the Happy Hunting Grounds. A likeable and reasonable deity.

Manitoulin island is located near the north shore of Lake Huron. It is the world's largest island in a fresh water lake. There's even a lake on the island. Is there another even smaller island on that lake? I don't know. According to Indian mythology, the island is the earthly abode of Manitou. Which is another original feature of the deity, I think. In Bohemia, I didn't think that Manitou might have a home on the Earth. True, the Greek pantheon shared Mount Olympus and the Norse gods lived in Asgard, but nothing similar has been encountered since. Christian temples are just metaphorical, symbolic homes of God. I hadn't heard of God having tangible property, real real-estate. But why not? The Creator of everything has the power to claim a particularly pleasant piece of countryside for himself. And Manitoulin Island is such a blessed place, full of rolling forests and meadows and lakes and fertile soil.

As a boy, I could only wish that one day I might have a peek into Manitou's domain. And what you know, I have, finding so many things that would have enchanted me back then, like a full ceremonial head-dress, a real bow and arrows, or a pair of moccasins decorated with porcupine's quills, just as I read about them in Karl May's books. I wish I was ten years old again! And I never imagined that I would actually pitch my tent in Manitou's backyard. Surprise! The fire flickers and cracks and smells the same way as it does in front of the cottage. The wieners frying above the flames at the end of a stick are not the variety sold in Bohemia, something called knackwurst, the beer tastes a bit different from Popovice lager, but the darkness around is quite identical with Czech darkness, the embers glow and warm you up in the same way too, and when you look up, the stars are the same as those over Chotouň. Enjoy camping in the realm of your childhood dreams.

Low Tide

The highest tides in world are in the Bay of Fundy. You can find such a sentence in just about every book of Jules Verne, that mentions sea, tides or sailing - waiting for the right tide to sail out of a harbour, getting Nautilus off the rocks in Indonesia, that kind of thing. Well, since there is a superlative tide, we should go and see it too. The Bay of Fundy separates southern Nova Scotia and New Brunswick.

We wanted to take a dip in an ocean. Wet our feet in the Atlantic, at least. Despite the rain. In our van, on a parking lot, with dunes hiding the beach from view, we changed into our bathing suits. Rain or no rain, we sprinted out of the van, up the dune. Saw the Atlantic ocean. Sort of. Within the visible distance – visibility quite limited by rain – we could see nothing but the wet yellow sand of the beach covered with seaweed, clams, mini-squids, crabs, minnows, jelly fish and who knows what else of Poseidon's rubbish. It smelled like fish. Quite a bit. So our feet didn't get their dip in the Atlantic. We didn't feel like zigzagging through those fruits of the sea, especially since we couldn't really see through the rain where the sea began.

Disappointment. Sure, the mistake was ours. We didn't think it through. The ten, twelve, even fifteen metre vertical waves mentioned by Verne, transform into two, three, even five hundred horizontal meters of sand. Five hundred metres of rather unsavoury view full of seaweed, all kinds of shapeless slippery creature, broken shells and other smelly jelly things. We should have expected that. Literature always distills the reality and writing about adventure and suspense does not distract the reader with descriptions of rotting crustaceans and pungent seaweed.

Satellite Dishes

Driving through South Dakota, Nebraska or Wyoming in the early 1990s, one noticed that many farms sported a big satellite dish. Sure, there was no cable available in the vicinity and residents wanted to be connected, informed, entertained. The dishes were not what surprised me though. Where else if not on isolated farms should they fulfil their function.

What I found more interesting was the fact that most of those dishes bore a colourful picture on the inside curve – an elk under the moon, a howling wolf, snowy rocky peaks - that kind of picturesque painting, obviously home made. The pictures pleased me. Not the quality - Impressionists and even most Starving Artists were miles above it - but the simple fact of their existence. They document the survival of the instinct for beauty, the creative impulse, the need to beautify one's surroundings. This need prompted the farmer or his wife to buy paint and brushes in town, get the ladder out of the barn, lean it against the dish and paint inside it whatever inspiration suggested. I had been tempted to believe that folk creativity was totally suppressed, defeated, displaced by mass-produced art; now I could see – not so fast, man, not so fast - otherwise I like the irony of the high-tech satellite dish serving as canvas for those amateur artists. The dish gave them access to prefabricated mass-produced art. These electromagnetic waves, with their encoded ready-made, mass art, were filtered through the most personal, hand-made expressions of the owner's personality. It seems as though artistic sensibility, the need for beauty and creativity, have much deeper and more resilient roots than I thought.

Two pubs

The Chotouň village pub was right next to our property. As a matter of fact, we shared a fence. The old pub was popular, especially on weekends, the goal of groups of citizens from the nearby city of Jilove, and on Saturday nights as a gathering place and watering hole for *tramps* on their weekly escape from Prague. It offered a large room with wooden floor boards, a dozen tables jammed together on a Saturday night, lots of light from six globe lamps floating in smoke and the smell of cheap cigarettes. No bar, just a tap counter and behind it a shelf with two or three bottles of liquor. All that was ruled by Hanka, the waitress, tap operator and cashier, in one four hundred pound personality.

Being such close neighbours, we would get the *tramps'* entertainment as if we were sitting inside with them. Two or three acoustic guitars, a couple of spoons for percussion and fifty to sixty voices. Enough for carrying a whole evening. Very popular was a song about the last stand of General Custer, beginning with the words:

Not far from Little Bighorn, there lies Indian land
General Custer rode there with his seventh cavalry

The chorus would sing this one several times during the night, and why not? It's not a bad song. After all, most of the repertoire reflected fascination with the American Wild West, with country and western music and the Czech counterpart – *tramping*. Occasionally, we would hear *Going West Ain't Easy Going*, too. It seems amazing how the history of one nation entered into folk lore on another continent, how American country and western music sprouted roots in Bohemia.

So I was ready, prepared, sort of, and on familiar territory, when, humming this song, I found myself driving within shooting distance of the Little Bighorn battlefield. I didn't visit the place. It might have been interesting to watch the battle itself, but I have no need to look at empty fields where butchery took place more than a century ago. Looking at those battlefields would be for me like trying to read a musical score instead of listening to a symphony. I pass the reading of strategic and tactical clues from the topography to a military professional.

It was a different matter when I dropped into a pub – called a saloon here – in Deadwood, Black hills, South Dakota. Yes, the very same saloon where Wild Bill Hickok was shot to death some hundred and twenty years ago. Believe it or not, this pub looked different from the one in Chotouň. Even looked different from the way I, sitting in the Chotouň pub, imagined a saloon. The lighting was so dim you had to wait few moments after stepping in from the sun-drenched street, to let your eyes adjust. Then you could make out a very long mahogany bar disappearing into the depths of the room, behind it long, shining rows of alcohol from all over the world, all reflected in a mirror behind them so they looked twice as numerous. Lots of harmonized, subdued colours. Very few customers, probably because it's still before noon. A smooth, polite barman.

I didn't order Popovice Billygoat beer as I would in Chotouň, though I wouldn't be all that surprised if they sold it here, but rather Jack Daniels whiskey on the rocks. I thought it befitting to my presence in a South Dakota saloon. I know, only unrespectable people drink liquor before noon, but I considered it the price of admission for enjoying the ambiance of this historic place. Yes, it is historic, because a historic personality was shot here. Though it's almost empty now and very quiet, I have no problem imagining Saturday night here. The line at the bar would be two deep, the talk flowing freely. Poker would be played here and blackjack there, somebody in vest and bowler hat might tickle the ivories of an upright piano.

And now, through the swinging doors a party of *tramps* from Chotouň would enter. What would they do? Would they be overwhelmed, as if in a sacred place, sit down quietly in a corner and look timidly around, whispering among themselves but still be delighted to be in a real saloon? Or would they regain their footing quickly, ignore the ghost of Wild Bill at the corner table, shout "another beer, Hanka", have a good gulp, wipe off the foam, and hit the strings of their guitars. If so, before they reached the third refrain, the whole saloon would be singing with them:

the Sioux tribe is courageous and knows their country well

I don't know what the *tramps* would do. Nobody does. Between heaven and earth there are mysteries that we can't solve. There's nothing to do but raise the Jack Daniels, toasting the alchemy of Art that manages to transmute the rough and raw blood and guts of history into an entertainment for folks living half a globe away.

Nautilus

Czechoslovakia is a landlocked country, her borders some three hundred kilometres from the nearest sea. Though the government once owned about half a dozen commercial ships, it had no military Navy, much less a submarine. No wonder I never saw any subs *in natura*. Of course, if the government had one, I would have no knowledge of it; it would be so secret that even the sailors serving on it wouldn't know of its existence. When every leaky washtub, as long as it was green and had an army inventory number, is top secret, just imagine the orgies of secrecy involving a sub. I mean, there was no way I could ever have seen any submarine.

Until I drove into Groton, Connecticut. The roadside sign promised that we could see, outside and inside, and even touch, the USS Nautilus, the world first atomic sub. Of course, we went there. We saw. We touched. We were utterly amazed, first by the fact that the US Navy allowed us to visit the sub, though it had been decommissioned a long time ago, and, second, with what we saw inside: nothing less than an atomic power-plant stuffed inside a sub, moveable under water. And it could launch missiles and torpedoes. And defend freedom.

Even Mr. Jules Verne himself would stare at this vessel with his jaw dropped. His imagination foresaw a sort of electric propulsion; the designers of this sub had to solve thousand of ordinary problems that Verne didn't have to concern himself with. Well, this Nautilus is much more than Verne could dream of. It is a huge monument to the imagination corrected by reality, the reality that insists you eat with your elbows very close to your body, that you barely fit into the loo, and when you want to roll on your other side you have to levitate sideways out of your berth, roll, and then levitate back in. All while sleeping. The guys who served here, from the captain to the newest recruit, deserve a tip of our hats.

There is no salon with original paintings, couches and a fountain, as in the original Nautilus, nor smoking room, organ, or huge window through which to observe underwater marvels. When it came to comfort, yes, Nautilus was the product of quite another world. Obviously, reality is an indispensable corrector of the imagination. Technically speaking, this vessel can do at least the same things as the real *Nautilus* – wait a second... why do I say *real* Nautilus. How could I think that this technological marvel of steel, computers, and the atoms that propel it, is somehow not-real, inauthentic, derivative - of what? Of a fiction, a myth, created in words by the imagination of a French writer? Is it because the names are identical? The fact that I encountered the fiction first? That reality hardly ever matches the dream?

What do you think? Honestly, what comes to your mind first when you hear the word *Nautilus*? The modern one or the literary one? I confess, but keep it under your hat, since I don't want to fall into the hands of psychiatrists, that for me somehow the more real sub is the one designed, built and captained by a retired Indian maharaja, known in exile as captain Nemo. Powerful and everlasting is the combination of imagination, great storytelling and the boyish capacity for dreaming.

Cody

Entering the city of Cody, Wyoming, on the left side of the highway you can see a yellow painted big box-store. It is full of saddles, rifles, cowboy boots, colts, lassos, embroidered men's shirts for work, dance or church, stetsons for good guys, bad guys, and everybody in between, belt buckles, hunting knives from the pocket ones to the huge grizzly-killers, lumberjacks shirts, not to mention jeans blue, black, or white. I'm sure you could buy a horse in the corral behind the store, too. You could enter stark naked and leave on foot or on horse as a hundred percent outdoorsman and seasoned adventurer. Like, say, William Cody, who I believe was born in this city and later became famous as Buffalo Bill. We spent about two hours in the store exploring – as if it was a kind of museum or exposition. How often can you encounter most of the props of your childhood readings, in one place! You had to guess their look and texture from approximate descriptions and illustrations in books. Here you can see them all, touch them all, smell them all. You can try how your head looks wearing a stetson, how it feels to wear the riding boots. You can heft a real colt in your hand, finger the leather on a saddle or the rope of lasso. I can attest that lassos are made from a thick and quite stiff rope – very unlike the old clothesline with which I couldn't capture even the back of an immobile chair. I suppose the store would let you do some shooting, if you wanted to. I didn't want to leave that huge box full of toys for the boys between ages nine and ninety nine. Another case of 'better late than never'. Having filled the blank spots in my education, I could enjoy a buffalo meat hotdog.

I don't know if the insight is connected with eating buffalo meat, but I have just realized that I am wrong. Buffalo Bill wasn't born here, he wasn't 'a son of this place', as the old cowboy books would phrase it; on the contrary, he was, so to speak, the city's parent, the city's progenitor. Founding Father and Mother in one. I know that speaking of founding of a city sounds strange. What founding? What are you talking about? Cities have been around since time immemorial, having naturally grown from towns and villages and hamlets. You don't establish a city just like that, just because you feel like it. There would be no order if any young wet-behind-the-ears hotshot without *gravitas* could establish a private city. Only the likes of Alexander the Great would be allowed to say 'Let there be a city' and the city of Alexandria rises on the shores of the Mediterranean. True, it used to be, back in antiquity, that some mythical hero like Aeneas or Romulus, could establish a city. In our day? Only Brasilia comes to mind, when the government wanted bigger and more beautiful buildings, but I'm sure the whole project had to be approved by countless authorities and took a long time to realize, so you can see that the concept of establishing a city in modern days is nonsense.

On the second thought, the phrase *'since time immemorial'*, in the case of European cities, means about a thousand, certainly not more than three thousand years. That's why their beginnings are shrouded in the mists of mythology. American history is shorter, quicker. Europe needed about five thousand years to develop from the neolithic to computers, America only five hundred. The city of Cody was established a hundred years ago, corresponding to a thousand years in Europe. But a century is too short an interval to allow for the dissolution of fact into a mother-load solution from which first legends and then myths grow to obscure the real passage of events. A hundred years back is nothing, you can still almost find a few eye-witnesses of the events. The events are still clearly visible and that's why my inner eye can see the following scene:

Colonel William Cody, with a party of friends, is returning from a hunting trip to Yellowstone Park. Just before sunset, reaching the last ridge before the valley opens up, he's overcome with the beauty of what he sees. He stops his horse, leans forward, pushes down his stetson to shield his eyes and says: "I see plenty of fertile black soil, I see the lush grass of green meadows, I see natural marvels right in our backyard, I see that this land has been blessed. That's why, in the midst of this plain, I see a city rising, not large but affluent, because the farmer tilling this land will need to buy a plough and scythe and sell the grain and tomatoes, the cowboy tending thousands heads of cattle will need to come on Saturday night to wet his whistle and dance with a local maiden, and the weary Yellowstone pilgrim will appreciate a roof over his head and a bed under his butt. May the city arise and flourish here and may its name be Cody. How. Amen."

And lo and behold, it came to pass and the city of Cody has flourished, as foretold, ever since. In five hundred, maybe a thousand years, when our days are shrouded in the mists of myth, when mice, bureaucratic reorganizations and the fires of history have eradicated any information about the person of William Frederick Cody, when even his tombstone will have turned into dust, everything will be the way it should be. The city of Cody has been here since time immemorial, established, according to local legend, by the mythical hero Beaufill or Buffalo. Future historians will create hypothesis about where the name Cody originated.

That will be the very time when the phenomenon called Buffalo Bill, for the first time, swings open the doors of the very special saloon, leans nonchalantly against the long bar, asks the ganymedes behind the counter for 'double nectar on the rocks', and looks at the faces populating the room to decide whether to flirt with Helen of Troy, shoot the breeze about marksmanship with Robin Hood, or talk hunting with Beowulf...

Kennedy Space Centre

"Impossible." The word sounded from the open door of the bus for the third time.

We had made it to the station a few minutes after the ticket office closed, but since the bus was still there, and half empty, I tried to negotiate the buying of tickets from this guide. If she had no tickets to sell us, I would pay her cash without getting any. I would do anything to get us aboard. We had come all the way from Ontario and had to leave tomorrow morning...

"Impossible!" The door slammed shut with a hiss.

Disappointment. Huge disappointment. We would not see the huge assembly building where the eagles nest on the roof, we would not see the launch-pads with the destination or gate sign saying: Moon. But I was far more disappointed by the state of NASA, by the fact, that something, anything, was impossible for NASA. Of all the organizations around the world, NASA is the last I would expect to hear this word from. I thought NASA had deleted the word from its vocabulary at its inception. A mere twenty years ago, it organized successful trips to the Moon for select people; today it's impossible to improvise a bit to accommodate three people who wish to participate in a tour of Cape Canaveral. Downfall, I couldn't call it anything but downfall.

When did the decline begin? Who knows, but maybe the answer could be found a few hundred meters away, at the entrance to the museum. On the lawn there was the Saturn V rocket. Felled. Lying on the grass instead of standing, of being the proud vertical, challenging the whole solar system. Gigantic, majestic, the masterpiece of von Braun, the biggest and the most powerful rocket ever built, the only vehicle, so far, able to pull man beyond earth's gravity, the only means of flying to the Moon. It delivered a few astronauts there a few times, back in the seventies.

Until a powerful senator came up with the opinion that all that progress was a waste of money. He convinced a few other senators and together they started to chip away, to cut and saw and chop the proud Saturn, finally managing to bring it down. First, they eliminated the planned Moon missions, then they stopped all the financing, not only for Saturn's further flights but for its development as well. Saturn V has been grounded ever since. Gutted, put into a museum as a thing that outlived its usefulness. Good for nothing anymore. To make things worse, the production and assembly lines were shut down and all the machinery and tooling was destroyed. The technology was demolished. So it would become exceedingly difficult, if not impossible to fly to the Moon ever again.

Well, to stop funding for a project so big that it can't be accomplished without government – that is the privilege of politicians, but ordering the destruction of what has already been built and paid for, seems stupid, senators, the real waste of money. Destroying the results of discoveries, of research, of knowledge itself, means robbing the common treasury of mankind. Such destruction has been considered barbaric – at least within Western civilization. Some other civilizations around the world perhaps value knowledge too lightly and are willing to destroy it either because of ignorance or in the name of some ism, but here, in America? Are not Discovery and Invention America's middle names? Has not America been built on the idea of permanent *progress*? Killing the

Saturn V project, destroying its fruits, is not only stagnation, it's *regression*, gentlemen. How far back would you like to go? Once you have started by dismantling Saturn V, how about the Wright Brothers flying machine, the Newtonian mathematical systems that enabled us to start thinking about the Universe at all. How about the heliocentric system of Copernicus? It is a very steep and very slippery slope, that you're on, senators.

We could slide down, very easily, back to the conviction that a flat Earth is the centre of the Universe. Occasional chance discoveries mentioning space flights would be treated by future historians as pure fantasy and interpreted as mythology. Von Braun would become a late follower of Daedalus and the astronauts would become colleagues of Icarus, falling in a fireball to the ground. And grandmothers would be begged for the umpteenth retelling of a popular fairy-tale called "How Neil Stepped on the Moon and Left his Footprint There."

Guanella Pass

"Long live poetry." He raised his beer bottle.

An unexpected toast among the thin growth of pines on the campground high in the Colorado mountains, but not completely illogical. We were resting in this deliciously wild camp after the long drive from Ontario. We were the only campers there. For some reason people were not flocking to the place that offered nothing but an outhouse and a tap with potable water. The only one other guest was this middle aged, tanned man with a stetson who arrived around noon. He found his spot not far from us and we could see that he was no greenhorn at pitching a tent or kindling a fire. Meeting at the water tap, we struck up a conversation. He was from San Francisco, high school teacher by day, poet by night. A published poet. He liked travelling, stepping out of the daily routine, away from running the mill, a poetic activity. We invited him to share our campfire, beer and talk.

A poet.... San Francisco... of course, poetry in San Francisco equals Beatniks. At least for me. He'd be about twenty years too young to be an authentic beat, but he couldn't have escaped their influence. Save for a few generalities, I didn't know much about the beat movement, though it used to be talked about quite a bit in Czechoslovakia. This man knew Ferlinghetti personally, while I knew no more than two or three of his poems in translation. Well, so be it, I'd take my chances, we might have a good talk without my embarrassing myself as a complete ignoramus. To stick to the few familiar facts, I asked him whether the City Lights bookstore still existed. I had heard about it in the sixties.

Oh yes, of course it did, still going strong, still offering the best and largest selection of poetry in San Francisco, still publishing the best poetry, still being the meeting place for poetry aficionados. Then he asked me how popular the Beatniks were in Bohemia, which of their books were best loved.

Well, how to put it... they were known as a phenomenon, as a legend of a kind, but they weren't published in Czech. That is, it was known that they rebelled against America and that was about as much as we knew. I suppose we rooted for them because every youth instinctively supports a rebellion. What they rebelled against, what they wanted, what and how they wrote, was inaccessible because... ultimately irrelevant. His forehead furrowed. He couldn't understand. I had to explain that in Czechoslovakia, back then, as in the whole Russian empire, the government assessed poets and artists in general in terms of their political and propaganda usefulness. The Beats criticized America, so that meant they were with the Russians, on the side of progress, and were presented as progressive, if not revolutionary artists. Of course, there were limits. Ginsberg, Kerouac, Ferlinghetti, those three represented the whole movement. Burroughs was completely off limits, disqualified first because of being the scion of a rich, exploiting family, second by being a homosexual and third for being an unapologetic drug user. No, the comrades couldn't use such an individual.

In the mid sixties, the first few translations were published in literary magazines, little bit of Ferlinghetti, most of Ginsberg. Ginsberg himself visited Prague, but failed to meet the expectations of the comrades and a little scandal ensued. The Party could tolerate and support progress of certain kind only, and only up to certain limits and homosexuality was way beyond those. What upset us high school students, back then, was the fact that he was expelled on the basis of private diaries that the secret police had confiscated, that is, on the basis of what he thought and not anything he did.

It was rumoured that Jack Kerouac had written a wild and scandalous book called *On the Road*. It enjoyed a great reputation without anybody actually knowing what it was about. When it was finally published – which must have been around 1978, thirty years after it was written and twenty after the original publication – we jumped at it, read it – and were a bit disillusioned. I don't know what we expected; wild parties, drugs, sex, porn, and who knows what else, I suppose. We were disappointed. On the basis of the snippets of information, and based on our own experience, we had thought that Kerouac was rebelling against the political control of the power system, of the state. Against lack of freedom. Having read and contemplated the book, our disappointment took on an angry edge. *Just look at him! He isn't working anywhere, running all over America on a whim, anytime he feels like it, and that still isn't enough for him, he's still dissatisfied! What with? He can do anything he fancies and still doesn't have enough freedom? Our Socialism would make short work of that! The authorities would have caught up with him after the first hundred miles, before he could make it to Pennsylvania, and lock him up for not working, for leading a parasitic way of life. What does he criticize? What's so progressive about him? What does the asshole want?*

"Nothing less than to unleash a gale of fresh air into the mustiness, the fartsy and stale morals that ruled the middle class America back then", he explained, "and to blow a good wind draft through a stale literature as well. *On the Road* was an influential book".

"Misguided and misguiding," I suggested. "Let's say that the dream of the beats came true and every citizen liberated himself to become a Beatnik, enjoying his or her limitless freedom on the road – I wonder who would cook their meals in the pubs, make their beds, manufacture those beautiful cars Kerouac so digs driving, sell him gas, pour his drinks in a bar and blow that wonderful jazz on a saxophone... I don't think they thought their rebellion through, though they weren't stupid."

He watched me attentively. "They weren't thinking in political or economic terms. They knew that poetry is poetry, society is a society and politics is politics. One doesn't mix them."

"Poetry, or Art, exists within a society", I responded. The words of poets do have influence. In the case of the Beats, their lives were influential as well. You can see the results of their influence all around you. Their extreme egoism, selfishness, without any regard for consequences. The praise and popularization of anarchy which gave rise to hippies in the sixties. The Beats weren't exactly strangers to drug use and its promotion either... Probably the anarchy is the worst thing, refusing any order and one's place in it... that's how cancer cells behave!"

"That's none of Kerouac's or Ginsberg's business. It's the business of society to sort out impulses from originating individuals, to chose which ones to adopt, tolerate, refuse or expel. True, sometimes a good impulse can go wrong. Such is the risk of freedom."

He could sense my disagreement. I wondered how he might see me? I considered him to be a bit naive. We remained in friendly silence for a while, sipping our beer. Then he pushed his stetson backwards and said slowly: "I think I know why we don't see eye to eye. I noticed your saying that your rulers assessed Art from a political point of view and you opposed it, but you're doing the same thing - from the opposite point of view, but essentially the same thing. They presented the

Beatniks to you as primarily a political force. You were rejecting Ginsburg and were disappointed with *On the Road* on the basis of politics. Not of Art, politics. I don't do that. Most people around here don't do that."

Bingo. Hammer. Head. Nail.

My forehead furrowed. Revision of this chunk of my old thinking has so far been eluding me.

No Name Wonders

Highway number 128 runs between Moab – the gateway to The Arches National Park – and Cisco, where it joins the I-70 which, in an eastern direction leads to Grand Junction. The highway winds through a deep and narrow valley, at times a canyon, at times only a gulch, of the Colorado river. The river is already of good size, though it still has another five hundred kilometres to run before charging into the Grand Canyon. The rocky walls of this canyon are dark red, the water is bluish as is the sky above, the trees dark green. Though we had already seen Zion National park, The Arches, Grand Canyon and other marvels of this corner of America, we're amazed at what we see along this highway. Nature has been prodigally generous around here, one beautiful view opening after another, twenty, fifty little and not so little marvels. Very few cars use this road. It has no stopping places, no viewing spots to get out of the car and admire the vistas. This canyon hasn't made the list of *must see* wonders. This canyon is not ranked in the superlative category. Driving along this road drove my patience, my tolerance, to the tipping point.

I protest. I shout: I like it here! It's not the first time we've driven into somewhere unknown where our jaw dropped in amazement, not having expected anything so beautiful or interesting or bizarre. The discovery is always something to make you wide-eyed. Despite our astonishment at this place, I had never heard or read anything about it. No guidebook mentions such places; they're omitted from the lists of wonders. Only the most this or the most that qualifies. Only the superlatives. America not only likes the superlatives; she demands them. If it is not the most of the best, don't bother me with it, it's a waste of my time. That seems to be the attitude.

I don't feel comfortable in this culture of superlatives. In sports or business it may be producing champions never seen before, but it is impoverishing at the same time. Comparatives are not interesting, comparatives are overlooked. My collection of experiences would be much poorer if I hadn't driven through this canyon. We have found plenty of places that only a few know about. Just off the cuff – the exit from the Bighorn Mountains near Ten Sleep, not only lake Louise but the whole highway between there and Jasper, the mountain road between Lillooet and Whistler, Mackinac bridge in Michigan compared to the Golden Gate, tens of kilometres along the north shores of the lake Superior, redwoods compared to sequoias, indeed most of southern Utah. Considering that only Utah has four National parks dedicated to sculptural rocks, how can not-so-famous places measure up? Anywhere else in the world, they would attract crowds of pilgrims, be tourist magnets of the first magnitude, the basis of the local economy. Not in America. Competition here is too fierce. When even Yellowstone canyon plays second fiddle to the Grand Canyon, the Black Canyon of Gunnison might not even make the orchestra. Aiming for a gold medal is an admirable goal, but now and then to appreciate, even just not to overlook, fifth or even tenth place can offer a big reward.

Green Province

The concrete or asphalt of the highway winds through a green trough, sometimes almost a tunnel. Wherever your sight falls, it sees green. After an hour or so, you start feeling that even the skies have a greenish tint. True, there's a wide variety of green hues to be seen, but still, green is green. At least in summer, when the leaves are on the trees. Trees, nothing but trees. Hundreds of miles – trees, infinity of trees. Green is restful and relaxing. The highway from Maine to St. John – trees, from St. John to Fredericton – trees. They run wild around here. The forest. The Primeval forest, not only by looks and impenetrability but by origins, too; it has grown here since the primeval times. Contrary to my expectation, this forest is not of a boreal kind, comprised of evergreens. It's dense and bushy beyond the possibility of finding any path through. Its wooden warriors, veterans and greenhorns alike, attack each other with their trunks, throwing their weight around, swinging at each other with their limbs, permanently arm-wrestling major branches, clinched into each other like wrestlers trying to force the opponents to their knees, all to claim a bit more sunshine for themselves. Everybody against everybody else. They must have blunted a lot of chainsaws. It must have taken incredible lot of lumber-jacking to build a highway here. It must be a daily struggle to prevent the forest from swallowing the road back up. The trees seem bent on revenge, to be on permanent counter-attack from beyond both ditches. You feel like Moses and his Israelites in a temporarily parted green sea. But green, dammit, is restful and relaxing! You can feel the energy of all those maples and oaks and beeches and ashes and whatever else their names might be, their powerful urge to charge upwards. I feel, no, I'm almost sure, that if I stopped at the roadside for a pee, before I could return to the car, a new tree would already be growing through its floor and out the roof. Breathe deeply – there's plenty of oxygen around. Green is restful and relaxing. Visit New Brunswick.

Air Density

You're rolling down the freeway in Nevada, doing a hundred and twenty and all of a sudden – an almost noiseless tap and two square inches of yellow smear explodes on your windshield. After a short while, another one, though this time maybe not yellow. I don't count the hundreds of little speckles, don't register all the mosquitoes, fruit-flies and other tinies. But before long, here we have to stop at a gas station just to wash the windshield. I don't know why it is that the most and the biggest insects of all America can be found in Nevada, along a freeway in the late afternoon.

The drive is long and the wandering mind offers various explanations of this anomaly. Maybe it has something to do with all those local secret Air Force bases, like Area 51. Maybe they round up and deport insects from those areas for security reasons. First – the bugs could jeopardize the super-secret aircraft in flight. Their speed of 2000 km an hour could smash even a very small bug into a pancake size splash and obscure the pilot's field of vision. Second – you can never be sure for whom a bumblebee, say, might be working. The insect eye is built to see everything around it, so you can keep nothing secret from it. The insect could see, hear, discover and ... spill the beans. So every bug has to be banished from such airspace in the name of state security. All those exiles boosting the density of insect per cubic meter in the non-secret parts of Nevada.

Forget it. I'm just kidding, killing time during the endless drive across Nevada.

Do You Speak BMW?

Though America didn't invent the automobile, she embraced the idea wholeheartedly, immediately recognizing its potential and finding in it her calling. No wonder, considering the expanse of the land. No wonder, considering the prices made possible by Henry Ford's mass production. In short – cars and America are synonymous. Big country – big cars. It was for good reason that every big car in Bohemia was called *amerika*. An American car has been a dream for many Europeans, though such cars are not exactly the most practical things to drive in Europe. It can happen that a big car gets stuck between the walls in a narrow street, can't pass a streetcar, can't find a parking spot, won't fit into any garage. Driving *amerika* in Europe is a dumb idea, but who cares. Driving *amerika* is a matter of prestige.

Having valued *amerika* so highly in Europe, a newcomer to America is surprised to see that American roads speak a lot German, Japanese and, recently, Korean. Especially around New York, Washington and, of course, California. Seeing a Chevy or a Ford on the freeways around Los Angeles or San Francisco is almost as rare as seeing a Rolls Royce or a Ferrari, even though those Euro-Japanese small cars aren't exactly the most practical size for America. Big cars can easily fail to see them and smash them to smithereens in collisions, small cars can disappear in a snow bank or even a bigger pothole. After a long drive, lets say across Kansas, the small car is gasping for breath and begging for a rest. So is the driver, agitated, shaken and battered. The small car is scared to be alone in your big garage, and is cold in there. Driving a Euro-Japanese car in America is a dumb idea. But who cares. It is *German engineering* and a matter of prestige. Why the engineering of nations soundly defeated by American engineering in WWII should become prestigious is beyond me. I guess prestige has more to do with advertising than with reason. Snobbery is completely irrational.

And so only in those parts of the land where prestige and snobbery do not play a role, as in the expanse between the Mississippi River and the California border, can you hear the honest American English of deep-throated eight-cylinders, the indefatigable pickup trucks and the comfortable full size sedans, made in Detroit. Tailor made, that is, for the size and conditions of America. This land requires big cars. Plenty of room everywhere, long drives to anywhere, winters quite harsh and summers too. The desire for comfort behind the wheel is nothing to sneer at. Let alone with a girl in the back seat...

In Europe, I would probably prefer a European car, but on this continent I definitely want a made-in-America *amerika*. You can trust me on this issue, I've experienced both. I used to drive a European made Ford Cortina in Czechoslovakia, in Canada I've indulged myself behind the wheel of a full size Ford Crown Victoria and her successor, now on my driveway, a Mercury Grand Marquise.

Temples

Time was when an ordinary church and its steeple was the highest structure in town and vicinity. You could see its clock from anywhere and find your bearings by looking at it. Gothic cathedrals still command respect and awe with their reach for heaven. The Lord. When you stand inside them. Looking at them from the outside you don't find them as dominant as they once were. Not even in Europe, much less in America, much less in big cities.

The church of Saint Peter and Paul in San Francisco has a nice white facade but isn't conspicuous by its height, not even in San Francisco, which doesn't have that many skyscrapers. The inside of this church looks like a common neo-baroque church, but the outside... I couldn't believe my eyes... that facade ends at the corner, the sides look like an ordinary office building, a box with a flat roof and rows of square windows. When did temple architecture disappear? Where is the cruciform ground plan? Colourful church windows? What's going on? Do saints Peter and Paul augment their income by renting part of this building to some office? Are they themselves renters? Who knows... one of the peculiarities of San Francisco.

Saint Patrick's cathedral, on Fifth avenue in New York, has slightly different problem. Though it is a full fledged cathedral, from the inside and outside, from the sides and back as well as from the front, though it is an impressive, majestic building, you don't feel it dominates its surroundings. Not in Manhattan. It can't compete with the mass of Rockefeller Centre, right across the street, can't rival the height of most surrounding buildings. Twenty, thirty floors. Looking from the top of the nearby Empire State Building you might overlook it. I wonder if it is visible from the heavens. Poor Saint Patrick. The temples of big money and big business are looking down at him. Down, from the hundredth or so floor.

In Washington, DC, the cathedrals would have a better chance to dominate the skyline if their height were not limited by a local law ordering that no building be higher than the Capitol. So only in smaller towns and cities is the church still one of the dominants. I suppose this situation reflects our times and the relationships between God, Mammon and Government.

everyday poetry

Do you know how many gems, I mean linguistic gems, are hidden in the high mountains and deep forests of Alberta and British Columbia, in places you might not visit unless you are a skier? They are hidden in ski resorts and are only visible against the white background of snow. They probably sleep over the summer. Follow me, I've been to some of those places and have noticed them. Being sensitive to the gems of the language is one privilege of a writer, so I can show you what I mean.

I have in mind the names of ski runs. In Špindl, in Bohemia, where I used to ski as a youngster, there were three runs – black, red, and blue. In the Canadian Rockies there are tens, even over a hundred runs in a single resort! Their best names are pure poetry, being metaphors that introduce the run in a word or two. They picture the run and the feelings of the skier about the run at the same time. Everyday poetry, so to speak. Maybe even a bit of an answer to those who ask what poetry is good for.

I think they encapsulate the feelings of the skier has who just finished his run, managed to stop at the bottom in a cloud of snow, panted and uttered: It made me sweat more than *Hell's Kitchen*, or it was worse than our *Schoolmarm*. When somebody says he skied down *Garbage Chutes, Elevator Shaft,*

Chimney, or *Freefall*, you are not likely to ask if it was steep. *Wildeside*, *Tightspots*, *Gunbarrel*, or *Intimidator* are suggestive enough. In the case that being scared beyond your wits is not your cup of tea but you still like some adrenaline rush, you might try *Rollercoaster*, *Adrenalin*, or even *Ecstasy*. If you prefer the delicious side of life, I can recommend *Eldorado*, *Short and Sweet*, *Single malt*, *Cleavage*, or even *Heaven Can Wait*. You may be delivered to the top of the mountain in angelic arms of the lift called *Angel Express*, on the way down you can enjoy *Angel Flight*. Just watch for the turn, or you might end up on *Fallen Angel*. I'm not kidding, angels are at home in ski resorts. More than one has a run named *Paradise*.

Now, if you will excuse me for a moment, before choosing your favourite run, I mean metaphor, I have to investigate the one at Sunshine Village that they call *Delirium Dive*.

Labrador

Maps do not lie, they say. Maybe not. But they can be misleading. Or at least distorting, especially if you overlook the little number, usually crouching somewhere in the corner, indicating the scale. But even it you notice and read it, it doesn't help much, because you don't know, can't imagine what, let's say 1 : 10 000 000, means. You may know, mathematically, that one centimetre on the map equals a thousand kilometres, but that still tells you nothing. You've never travelled a thousand kilometres. A thousand kilometres is more than the whole length of Czechoslovakia.

You've been flying for three hours over the Atlantic Ocean when the plane starts to bump up and down, to hiccough as it hits turbulence. Experienced fliers conclude that we're crossing the divide between the ocean and the land. Inexperienced ones, like us, are told so by the pilot. We feel better. For some reason lots of people believe that in the event of a lost wing or detached engine, it's better, somehow safer, to crash among evergreens than to splash down in cold, salty water.

So, you stretch and relax, and then start fussing about, believing that once we're over the land, we'll be in Toronto in no time. Pretty soon we're going to begin our descent and final approach. Better put on your shoes and take out your coat, because now everything will go fast. To avoid looking completely silly, you check the expected arrival time. What? Three more hours? How come? We're already here, in America, in three hours we must be at the Rockies. Will we be circling around and around the airport? Is my watch going too slow? Are they kidding?

You look out the window and you can see that the pilots are not kidding. You're still flying straight ahead. Down there, you can see the thin forests of Labrador and slightly denser forests of Quebec, one hour, two hours and we are still not over Ontario. What distances! Down there, you see nothing but forests – for two hours nothing but trees, no town, village, road, not even a farm with smoke from the chimney, nothing to indicate a human presence. Maybe there are some footprints on a trap-line in the first snow but they are invisible from ten kilometres above. Two hours at 900 kilometres per hour makes 1800 kilometres. You could fit most of Europe into a circle of this diameter. In here – no sign of humans. Oh my, how big is Canada when we can afford to leave such a huge expanse uncultivated, even totally uninhabited?

Scribner's

New York has lots of sights to see, but, oddly, my thinking has been triggered by a small plaque next to the door into a large store that announces the former location of Scribner's sons publishing house. It was on Fifth avenue, somewhere around Fiftieth street, I think. Of course, two names come to mind immediately: Francis Scott Fitzgerald and Ernest Hemingway. I can almost see them at that moment emerging from behind the corner in animated conversation, both of them young, and both a little tipsy. They enter through the glass door, climb the stairs to the mezzanine, presumably to visit Max Perkins, their editor, in his office. To the house that made literary history, by way of historically important door, off that historic sidewalk. When they disappear, I look around me, first through the eyes of their books and then with my own eyes. I notice that New York as I see it today is different from what their descriptions generated in my mind. Not their fault, mind you; the transfer to Prague just changed the background against which my mind was imagining.

Somewhere, Fitzgerald is describing a girl sitting at the window, watching the opposite windows. Simple image, isn't it – and yet, you're off the mark. Not all windows are created the same. The New York window is vertical, opens by sliding up, Prague windows have two wings and open like a door. Prague windows can't guillotine you, the New York window can't bang or slam shut in a burst of wind. You have blinds as opposed to curtains. The facade with a set of windows makes a quite different impression in New York than in Prague.

Another example – somebody is walking on a sidewalk, stepping carefully. The scene is nicely described, you can all but hear his shoes squeak. If you were a Czech reader, you would automatically imagine a sidewalk paved with little red, blue and grey cobblestones, a background generally merry, while the monotony of grey concrete in New York can suggest a blue mood, even depression. The shop signs are different, as are steps to the doors and the doors themselves, even lampposts; in short, the whole street is different. Reading, you are projecting the story onto the familiar backdrops, following your New York heroes as if they were living in Prague, as if their actions were taking place in Prague streets. OK, when it comes to backdrops like streets or windows, who cares, right? Well, how about the unstated backdrops of mental life, about morals like windows with different curtains, about conscience treading different sidewalks? About freedom?

Whether you like it or not, whether you fight it or not, you are misled a bit, because with a good translation you expect to be getting hundred percent of the work. No way. As you view a foreign literature through the telescope called translation, there is, in its optics, among the lenses of the telescope, a tiny surface of built-in mirror, a bit of your own mind that supplies images from the reservoir of the known, familiar, experienced. The mirror may be reliable and truthful enough in the case of domestic authors, but it distorts when aimed across a border, into a foreign literature. Like a prism, those inter-literary borders somewhat bend and split the rays of light, painting in the mind of the reader a picture slightly different from that described by the author. Difficult is the life of the translator.
Should we skip reading in translation altogether, then? Nonsense. Better to meet *Gatsby* or the *Old Man and the Sea* in translation than to miss them. It's just a good idea to

realize that there are limits to what you are receiving, that the received picture may not be completely identical with the original. But maybe you have to visit New York and run into Messrs. Hemingway and Fitzgerald, conjured by the sign of Scribner's sons, to realize such things.

Pine tree

I have no idea how far past Sault St.Marie that little island in a little bay of Lake Superior was. But it was about ten by ten metres, a pile of rocks and stones. On its top there stood, or, better, twisted, a pine tree. Its branches were driven and combed by wind to be almost horizontal, like a girl's hair in the breeze. The overall impression was, in a word – torn up. Just like a painting of one of the Group of Seven. Literally, as if the painting came alive, as if the pine I saw was a copy of the painting. I mean what I say, the painting having preceded this pine, having been done at about the time when this pine was still a seed in a cone. The artists just painted a grandma of this pine, making her archetype of pine. Art students should be brought here to show them which is the model and which the work of Art. To see artistic transformation, and share something of the artist's mind in painting his canvas.

What I realized, looking at this tree, was the need for the modification of impulses transplanted from a native soil into any not-so-native one. Transplant Monet here, from the blossoming French meadow, let him erect his easel among these stones, and if it doesn't get blown away, the resulting painting, while still being a Monet, will fall short of doing justice to this island and this pine. Something will be missing. Maybe the attacking and high splashing waves, minus thirty five degrees in winter or plus thirty five in summer, unheard of in France, maybe the gales, roughly three times more powerful than anything he had witnessed at Fontainbleau or Giverny, the lashing and bombardment by snowflakes driven by a blizzard... to make a long story short, Monsieur Monet would have to understand the life story of this pine to capture her essence with his brush.

When members of the Group of Seven discovered Monet and the other Impressionists and tried to apply their technique to painting the Canadian landscape, they quickly discovered that French Impressionism had not enough breath, range or musical scale to capture the larger-than-life size fates of Canadian pines on lake Superior. They understood that if they wanted to paint truthful paintings they had to change the status of Impressionism from visitor to immigrant, to plant it in the local soil, let it infuse and soak into the rough and tumble of the Canadian experience. Glory to them for doing it, creating something wonderfully Canadian and supremely Artistic at the same time. And, without really meaning to, just offhand, they offered us a blueprint for dealing with all artistic impulses coming from overseas.

Workhorses

When I was a boy of about four, deep in the fifties, I could often see two horses in the streets of the Prague neighbourhood called Smichov. They were massive, a bag of oats hanging around their necks, harnessed to a small blue delivery wagon with the Post trumpet painted on its door. In a year or two, they disappeared; pushed off the stage by station-wagons; they clip-clapped away into the twilight of history.

Not until I made it to America did I see a horse working in the streets of a city again. In the nineties. Not in some god-forgotten western place, where time stopped a hundred years ago, no, it was in no less a place than Washington, DC., within sight of the White house. Even more remarkably, it was right in front of NASA headquarters, that is, in the very epicentre of the scientific world, where time is running so fast that it outruns itself. He, the horse, was clopping slowly and deliberately past a long row of parked cars. If I had seen a pink dinosaur in a tuxedo and top hat riding a scooter, I wouldn't have been more surprised. A policewoman was riding the horse. Despite his rider, the horse had no siren, no flashing lights between his ears or underneath his tail. Nor a bag of oats. They moved with very old fashioned slowness. Now and then, stopping the horse, or maybe he stopped on his own, she scribbled something for a while, then leaned far sideways and inserted a ticket behind the wiper-blade of a parked car. It seemed to me that the horse always threw his head sideways, as in triumph, and laughed gently. I guess, he was addressing the car: now you see it, you heartless pile of metal, you pushed me from the stage of history but I am back, because in this big city I am more practical than you, and now I am going to settle that historical injustice. I am going to make you pay! And I enjoy it... you know, having the last laugh...

Davenport

Many years ago, we had enjoyed a wonderful dinner in a family restaurant in the city of Davenport that lies on the Mississippi river, right on the border between Iowa and Illinois. Now, we were driving in the vicinity again and our stomachs were chiming the time for lunch, On the last day of our vacation, we deserved a good square meal, didn't we? But, how did we get to that restaurant last time? What was its name? More heads – more reason, they say. Our three heads produced three suggestions. We agreed that the exit would be number one, three, or six, from off freeway loop around the city. We quickly discovered that number six was not the right one. Nevertheless we kept going to enter the city. We would follow our nose. It must have successfully detected the sweet smell from that restaurant because when, acting on instinct, I turned left after three kilometres, and then once more left, I found myself in a street that seemed vaguely familiar. Indeed, after another few hundred metres we were on the spot. Just coming from the other direction.

Around lunch-time a line of hungry would-be customers stretched right outside the door; an unmistakable sign that the place still offers marvellous cooking. The same fact was attested to by the much higher than average number of people who were chubby, plump, rotund, bulky, tubby, puffy, stout, full figured, obese, or outright fat. If additional testimony were needed, there was the slow waddle to their cars of people who had already eaten. Some of them had to move the seat back a notch or two to fit behind the wheel. Well, where else should you get a really good square meal if not in this farmers' land.

Within an hour, we were sitting down at a table. The waitresses had lots of fun when we told them that we found them by smell this time. They laughed. But I was serious. To use a map or, these days, even a GPS, you have to know precisely where you are going, the name, the address. Unless you're totally exact, all the technology can lead you nowhere and you go hungry. In such a case you have to allow the atavism of the hunter in you to lead you, to trust your instincts, your nose. It appears that it can at least direct you to a meal, especially if it happens to be one as good as those they serve here. They pampered us, insisting that we try a bite of this and a bit of that, and the cook sends his regards and this speciality as his personal gift for you, and don't forget pie with ice-cream to top it all off. It was a very delicious super-stuffing. Two notches on the car seat. We could and we did drive the whole afternoon and through the night, all the way home, in one go. I can't share with you the name of that restaurant, I have forgotten it again with a clear conscience. I know that if I ever drive around Davenport again, I can close my eyes and still find that place

Moose

Not long before our emigration, we visited the Museum of Nature in Prague with our small son. As we were walking among the collections, all of a sudden we froze as if we had seen the devil. From a niche in the wall a mounted moose head jutted out. A huge moose head. An unbelievably huge, hairy, antlered moose head. *The King of the Canadian North*, the caption told us. Good Heavens, this is a monster... do we really want to go to the land where it lives? Well, we did go there. After a while we even tasted moose meat goulash at our friends. They go hunting moose up in northern Ontario every fall. It's not that far, six, seven hundred kilometres. We weren't looking for the monster, so it took about twenty years before we faced it. Literally, face to face.

We were driving up a dirt road to scout out the ski resort called Whitewater, famous for its powder skiing. It's not far from Nelson, BC, just a few kilometres along the highway, then turn left on a dirt road. The uninhabited wilderness around us was in full swing, bursting with all its lush summer powers. We turned a corner and almost ran into a hairy mountain of meat, topped with antlers. A moose. Watching us. Taking the measure of us. Pondering whether we were a danger. He turned and took a few steps. I followed his hunches. He stopped, turning his head. I stopped. He moved. I followed. The ditches were full of greenery, but they were not steep, he could step aside easily.

He didn't feel like it. After all, he's on his home turf in these woods, we're the intruders, probably disrupting his lunch. I revved the engine a bit. He started to move faster. Perhaps his pace might even be called running. Most animals are enviably elegant when moving fast. Not so the moose. He looked like a clown trying to run in his huge shoes, swinging from side to side, his butt shaking in a clumsy counter-movement, his legs extending as if disjointed from the knees down, his hooves kicking out side-ways. It wasn't a run, it was a parody of a run. Despite being so massive, he didn't look menacing, as, say, a running buffalo would, but rather laughable. At least as long as he was running away from us. It didn't look like long cross-country gallops in equine manner were his cup of tea. It would be very hard to imagine him making an escape with a huge gracious leap like that of an antelope. No, graciousness was definitely not one of his strengths.

It crossed my mind that he might be delaying us deliberately, to amuse us, that he was a moose – comedian. He stopped, catching his breath. Judging by the antlers, he must have been an older gentleman. An elderly King of the Canadian North. We rewarded him with applause. I realized that we were witnessing something unique - a king with a sense of humour, even a king comedian.

Since time immemorial, kings and majesties of all kinds have had no sense of humour. They cannot afford to have a sense of humour. Majesty has to be serious as a grave stone, or it's not considered majestic. Humorous majesty is the king of all oxymorons. Since the dawn of history Power and Humour haven't seen eye to eye. They couldn't, being mutually annihilating. Humour humanizes, Power dehumanizes. Since the days of cavemen, it has been common for a plebeian joker to come up with an anecdote about his potentate, to humanize him a bit for his fellow citizens, and the potentate, instead of doing something for his health and laughing heartily, to get pissed of, to slam the joker with *lese majeste* behind bars. The better the joke, the stronger the bars. What can you do...

Moose looked at us. We bowed deeply, Your Artiodactyl Highness. Take your time. He straightened up to his full height, looking straight at us. We showed him thumbs up. He made a slight bow with his antlers. Then he turned and left the road, heading to the creek to have a drink. Must have been thirsty after all the exertion and excitement. Well, that's it… until the next time, Your Ruminant Majesty…

Prairie Campground

He was sitting in the open door of an old battered camper, wearing just shorts and a greasy stetson. Across his knees he held a big axe that he was sharpening. From the bushy beard hiding half of his face, a thick red-glowing cigar was sticking out. The manager of this campground, one of the very few in this part of Saskatchewan. It was situated on a small hill, densely covered with trees, another rarity on the prairies. It could be a good camp, not overly civilized. The guy looked like a *tramp* in both Czech and Canadian meaning of the word.

"Put up your tent anywhere you want to, nobody's here yet, it's our first season, few people know about us. Wood for fire? The more you take, the happier I'll be. You can have this axe, if you want, and you can fell as many bushes as you wish, it'll help me to clear the place. We haven't finished installing the pipes for potable water yet. If you're thirsty, grab a beer from this box and if you insist on water, give me your container and I'll bring you some from the town."

With his tanned bulk filling the door of his caravan, his bearded face talking and puffing on his cigar, he looked like an early settler, a pioneer from a hundred years ago, sitting proudly on the front steps of the log house he had built with his own hands and this axe.

Two hours later he brought us the water, lit another cigar and talked a bit more. He wasn't a tramp. He wasn't an original settler. He was a successful lawyer from Saskatoon. This spring he pulled the plug of his phone, put a sign, *Back in the fall*, on the door of his office and came here to have a rest. He's watching over and running and improving the campground for his friends. "It's like a paradise here. I wake up with the sun, I go to bed with the sun, no phones, no clients, no stashes of official documents, no stupid social conventions. It's so quiet here, I'm suntanned, I don't have to shave everyday, or wear a white shirt and a tie, I wash myself when I feel like it, can smoke anytime and anywhere, I can talk in the vernacular, even curse if I want to, nobody can hear me but the trees and sky... Try to do just ten percent of that, just once, in a courtroom... To put it simply, I found the freedom here that I had forgotten existed. Well, the more civilization, the less freedom. These are the best holidays I've ever had, holidays from the tyranny of my successful self."

Mess Tin

The Florida Epcot centre has just finished its fireworks and laser show, crowds of people are pouring out of the gates, finding their cars, driving away. We are facing a drive of 70 kilometres, and are almost shivering at the end of January, so we decide to warm up with chicken noodle soup before leaving. We take out the propane stove, put on it my mess tin filled with water. Before it comes to boil, I can tell you its story.

This mess tin is a veteran, true memorabilia, since it contains quite a bit of my life. At the very beginning of the first year of high school, all students had to participate in a three week 'work brigade'. We were forced to manually pick hops, getting paid peanuts, though hops was called green gold because it made so much hard currency for the government. Everybody had to have his own mess tin, as the food was ladled into it. No mess tin, no eating. You carried your mess tin with you all the time, just as you had a spoon in your pocket. This is where my mess tin and I started growing affection for each other. We repeated the hops picking experience two more times. Since then, it has travelled with me anywhere I needed a portable dining room. I was taking it to the cottage, to tenting holidays, to the ski trips, even on military service in case I might need a backup tin. So it's no surprise I brought it with me when we defected and it served us faithfully then; in Vienna, we would have had a hard time making a cup of coffee without it.

It goes without saying that the mess tin crossed the Atlantic with me and landed in Canada. I could see, I could feel, that it was flourishing here, as if experiencing a second youth. And no wonder. It must be the dream of any camping equipment, especially equipment made in Czechoslovakia, to camp in America's woods, to cook tea on the prairies of South Dakota, goulash in a canyon in Utah, or noodle soup in Florida. Back then, in Epcot, it was thirty years old. Now it's almost fifty, a veritable patriarchal age for a mess tin, but it's still going strong, is still industrious, still keeping itself in good shape. If we ever part, it will be because I've taken it to Alaska to bury somewhere near the Klondike, as this is where Czech tramping folk-lore located camping heaven. But that is in the distant future. For the time being it stands on the stove, bubbling contentedly, acting as a whirlpool for noodles. It's nice to carry with you something from your youth, something representing such long continuity.

End of talk, the soup is cooked. We will eat. Or will we? The huge parking lot is almost empty by now, save for us, sticking out in the middle of it. We must look suspicious. A car with a light bar on its roof is heading towards us. Must be the police. Find our passports, quick. They'll ask for them, interrogate us, confiscate our soup... But they don't demand any ID though they are from Disney security, just asking if we are having trouble and offering their help. They wish us bon appetite when they hear about the soup. I really thought there would be some trouble as there would have been in Czechoslovakia. Well, from his youth in Bohemia one brings not only a mess tin but also various reflexes and habits. A change in locale turns them into bad habits. Unlike a mess tin, they do you a disservice. They are good for nothing, but can't be easily uprooted and buried.

Edwards

When I stopped at the gate of Edwards Air Force Base, rolled down the car window and stuck my head out, the heat almost pushed me back. From a guard house, a soldier in fatigues emerged. Sure, he would let us pass to see the museum on the base, but we would have to have a permit. The permit is not difficult to obtain, it only takes two days. We didn't have that much time, so we had to be content with seeing the place from a distance. The soldier saluted, retreated into his air-conditioned guard-house. Poor kid, he must have been ecstatic when he received posting to Edwards, the legendary Edwards, without realizing how murderously hot this middle of nowhere is. The Mojave Desert. Heat that would mummify anything alive within a day. A dry lake bed. Of course it couldn't be anything but dry in this heat. A desolate place. That's why they built an air force shooting range here during WWII, then used it as an Air Force base, and finally transformed it into the Air Force research and testing facility. Since the end of the WWII, until the mid eighties, everything of importance happening in the US aeronautics happened here, from the breaking of the sound barrier to the landing of space shuttles. Famous place. Almost mythical. Speed records. Altitude records. Permanent pushing of the envelope. As one imagines all the white contrails rising and arcing into the blue skies, in this shimmering heat it seemed as if a cathedral was arising, reaching from this dry lake all the way up to the dark gates of the Universe, a cathedral dedicated to science and technology, to the faith in science and technology that is one of the religions of America. Her twins are touching the skies at Cape Canaveral, the Massachusetts Institute of Technology, Los Alamos, or, say, Menlo park of prophet Thomas Edison fame.

In the category of technical inventions, I underwent a correction of my knowledge early, in this case while still in school. In our very first textbooks, grade four or five, we learned the names of famous inventors, Russian names: one Polzunov, a self educated muzhik, invented a steam machine; another muzhik, Jablockov, invented an arc lamp; and A. S. Popov was mentioned as the inventor of radio. Well, in those days it was necessary to follow the ideology and promote the abilities of working class people, especially of Russian origin. There were more names in that textbook, but I mercifully managed to forget the rest. Two or three years later, those names were discreetly moved to their rightful positions of "also ran", and replaced with the names of the real inventors. All that experience taught me that authorities, even school textbooks, are to be taken with more than a grain of sceptical salt.

What I could understand only on this side of the Atlantic, is why America has been the place where inventive abilities exploded, and the number of inventions went through the roof, why inventiveness is a big part of American mental set up. The main ingredient of any inventive activity is freedom to do and to think your own way. Freedom to fail. Tolerance for the freedom of others. The freedom to thumb your nose at the authorities. All that promotes the can-do attitude. Every inventor, no matter how loony, can work on any idea, no matter how loony. One of them will work. Very fruitful philosophy. It probably originated with the Founding Fathers, especially Ben Franklin, who liked to fly kites during thunderstorms. Not long afterwards Sam Morse revolutionized the information industry with his telegraph. Is there any wonder that such examples inspired people? The natural human passion for discovering, the urge to push the envelope and the creative drive most of all, found in freedom its ideal partner.

The nature of the ninetieth century channelled this creativity into the natural sciences and technology. In the spirit of Titanism, inventors were challenging the gods themselves, showing that the World could have been created a bit differently, that creation can be improved upon, re-created. The times preferred action over contemplation. After the American Civil War, the golden age of inventors dawned. Before the end of the century the doors at the patent offices were permanently jammed. Maybe that was the inspiration for inventing the revolving door. There was a permanent race towards the brass wicket bearing the sign Patents, metaphorical and sometimes literal races. Now and then, in the street leading to the patent office, you might see a racing inventor, his beard flying, one hand holding his bowler hat in place, the other grasping a roll of blueprints. Inventors had to hustle, they had to run, they could never be sure that a competitor – even in another city – wouldn't be emerging from the other corner of the street, running for his life, trying to beat him to the wicket. They had to be in very good physical shape. America was so rich in talent that now and then faster legs might mean a difference between a million and nothing. Look at them, all dashing again... who's going to win this time? Edison or Tesla or Marconi or Bell, or one of those who managed not to stumble this time around? Healthy mind in a healthy body, as the ancient Latins used to say.

The same goes for their heirs, like Henry-the-Assembly-Line-Ford, or William Semiconductor Shockley, who has so decisively helped to shape our computerized world through his discovery. It might well be that one of the forces propelling all those discoveries and inventions is American restlessness, the penchant for adventure, for moving in and mapping out unfamiliar territory. So instead of grabbing a gun and reaching beyond the backyard into the wilderness, such an inquisitive spirit, say a scientist, may sit down with a microscope and a notebook, wondering what surprise the atoms and molecules have prepared for him today. Look at them, they form a double helix! And he starts wondering why? Still, nobody is making fun of him, nobody's tapping his forehead insinuating that when the scientist grows up it will be a huge relief for him and his loved ones too. If he likes to tinker with the double helix, let him tinker. Well, the scientist did his tinkering, packed his tuxedo, travelled to Stockholm to collect his Nobel prize. And inspired thousands of others to follow the adventurous path of discovery.

Back to Edwards and the nautics in the air. In this branch, too, inventors followed their own thinking rather than paying attention to the opinion of authorities. Luckily, the Wright brothers had never read the published conviction of experts pontificating that heavier-than-air objects could never fly. Nowadays, who knows, maybe here at Edwards they would be testing the newest, state of the art balloons, blips and zeppelins. I would love to see a streamlined rag zeppelin with rocket propulsion break the sound barrier... It was broken, right here, by a descendant of Wright brothers' Flyer, an aircraft nicknamed Orange Beast developed at Bell laboratories. Other silver birds ascended so high that a pilot could extend his arm out the window and knock right on the door of Space. In the end, all this development culminated in Wehrner von Braun, whose creation, considerably heavier-than-air, flew through air-less space all the way to the moon and back.

Would we have made it to the moon if it weren't for the attitude symbolized by Edwards? Probably, but the development might have taken different routes. Human passion for discovery, the vertigo of imagination and creation, would have invented other wings.

Golf Plots

In the sixties and seventies, you could find no more than five golf courses in all of Czechoslovakia. They were surviving from before the communist takeover, owing to the fact that an occasional western tourist, visiting Karlsbad or Marienbad spa, insisted on playing golf. The comrades needed hard currency more than they hated golf. Without prejudice, I have to admit, that their hatred might have been somewhat justified. In their own minds, at least. They knew, from their impeccable intelligence sources, that the game of golf was nothing but camouflage. What was really going on was based on the undeniable fact that golf was a game of the extremely rich and extremely powerful. Any golf course was a meeting place of cigar smoking big bankers and industry captains with generals and admirals – who smoked pipes – and with an occasional cigarette puffing politician or spymaster. Usually, they played in top-hats but that didn't matter as they were not hitting balls with clubs, oh no, they were fomenting plots. A golf course was in reality a plot hatchery. Our comrades hated any plot they weren't fomenting themselves. Of course, the golf course plots concerned the downfall of communism during the cold war, and that would mean the downfall of our comrades as well. Imagining that he might fall from the pinnacle of power and land on his face in the mud of everyday life is enough to drive any comrade insane. No wonder, then, that he orders the ploughing up of any existing golf courses, the planting of corn over fairways and cabbages on greens? To allow a few golf courses to operate, considering those circumstances, must be seen as outright philanthropy. Why the imperialists should hatch their plots in the fresh air of a golf course instead of the air-conditioned board or war-rooms, our comrades didn't tell us. Maybe their tobacco smouldered more tastefully in fresh oxygen.

Such was my mental set in the matter of golf that I brought with me to Canada. Sure, I quickly learned that there were several golf courses in London. Why not, rich and powerful people must live around here. Then I discovered that one of my colleagues at the Ford plant carried a set of golf clubs in the trunk of his car. Strange. Over time, I ascertained that about quarter of Ford workers are golf aficionados. Very strange – if they are so rich and powerful to play golf, what in hell are they doing on the Ford assembly line?

It was the numbers of the players that turned me around in the end. The circumstances and common sense offered two likely possibilities. One – in Canada, golf is a popular sport and, thanks to the high standard of living, is available to masses. Our comrades were lying. Two – the rich and powerful have their human moments too, and want to leave their board rooms and war rooms for a bit of golf in the fresh air. And our comrades, perish the thought, were lying even about such trifling matter as golf.

Still, I wasn't quite ready for what I ran into in southern British Columbia. We were driving from Kamloops to Kelowna, or it might have been from Kelowna to Cranbrook, or both, I can't remember exactly, and there was a sign along the road saying Golf club So and So. A few kilometres down the road another one. And another one. Every few kilometres was a golf course, sometimes even more than one. Who's playing here, I wondered. Those courses were twenty, sixty, eighty kilometres from the nearest town. A splattering of golf courses in the forested mountainous wilderness. Maybe the moose and grizzlies play here. Have the Bigfoot – or would it be Bigfoots or even Bigfeet – developed a passion for playing golf and for congregating in club houses as their social centres? I don't know, but I think there were at least three times as many golf courses along that highway as there were cities, towns, hamlets and solitary log houses. Maybe more than inhabitants.

But, who's working here to maintain the courses when not enough employable people are living in the vicinity? Do they hire mountain goats to keep fairways trimmed, wild rabbits to service the greens and deer to control rough? Or perhaps there are communities of people secretly living around those courses, modern day hermits who seek isolation to practice meditation and self-discovery. The other possibility that comes to mind is that those courses are family operated and that they co-operate with each other. Let's say on Monday morning several families work together on one course and then play in the afternoon, on Tuesday they move to the next family's plot, and so on. Unless it's a kind of self-serve golf course – come, get behind the wheel of a mower, cut your grass and then play for half price…

In the end, my guessing completes the circle and returns to the plot hatching hypothesis. Perhaps these might be reserve courses, in case New York and Washington and Toronto were attacked and strategy called for back up headquarters for the chief intriguers. Hatching a plot and a golf course are synonymous, aren't they? Another possibility might be that some of the super-rich and super-powerful couldn't stomach the end of the cold war, couldn't live without it, so they abandoned their mansions to start a guerrilla war, moving to sod houses and caves deep inside those forests to keep fomenting their intrigues in secret. Who knows…

Many mysteries indeed are hiding in the interior of British Columbia.

Monsieur Breton Would Smile

How can you tell that you are moving through an area called Near North in Ontario? Simply. Have a look at general stores and trading posts along the highway. There might be a gas bar as well, but it's not necessary. The main indicator is a big sign with advertising. Through the process of logically random additions, an original poem was created. Though it is an authentic expression of folk creativity, the poem is pure surrealism:

> *Pepsi Cola*
> *Live bait, minnows,*
> *Ice-cream*
> *Boats for rent*
> *Fresh eggs*
> *Worms*
> *Home-made pies*
> *Ice*
> *Lotto 6/49*
> *Help wanted*

Of course variations are possible. I even saw a very poetically enviable combination of *sheep-skin* and *amethysts*. I should make it farther up north one day. I might find things like *taxidermy, snowshoes, traps, blueberries, ammo,* and maybe even *we buy gold dust and nuggets*. I don't know what surprises might wait there, not knowing how the daily life might be shaping far north poetry.

Blueberry Art

Speaking about poetry, about the artifacts of art, brings to my mind a happening, or whaddyacallit, that occurred on highway 7 between Ottawa and Peterborough. A few dozen kilometres beyond the fields and meadows west of Ottawa, the highway plunged into an evergreen forest. We noticed a handmade sign, *Blueberries for Sale*. Nothing out of ordinary in this forest, in blueberry season we thought. Similar sign a bit further down the road. And another, and this one was on top of a tall spruce. The next *Blueberries for Sale* sign shone in white paint from the top of a nearby rock, then fluttered on a flag fixed to the chimney of an abandoned farm, was printed on a bed-sheet stretched across the road, decorated the side of a half collapsed barn some 200 metres from the road, hung from the hook of a parked crane. We felt the intent. We started suspecting a method in this craziness. We started to play the game. Where might the next one be? On a long pole sticking out of a little pond. Yes, there definitely was intent. You realized that advertising was not the primary purpose of this game; creating a work of art was. Somebody did all the work of thinking about it, finding the most impossible places along the fifty kilometre stretch and putting the signs in them. The entertainment of the drivers must have been the effect in his mind. Fun. His and theirs. It's an artist we're dealing with here. Sale of blueberries? Not a chance. Two or three berry huts along the road were not only closed, but actually bordered up. What we encountered here was pure Art for the Art's sake.

Changing of the Guard

Parliament Hill, Ottawa. 10.00 am. Down the street marches a square of red coats with white belts and huge bearskins on their heads. A marching band is giving rhythm to their steps. Right turn! Keep marching on the lawn in front of the parliament building. Stop. Tourists surround the lawn, cameras are clicking. Checking out the unit of guards before their duty. The buttons, the tightness of the belt, the closeness of the shave, the shine of the boots, the brushing of the bearskins. Check the cleanliness inside of gun barrels. The guns are not contemporaries of the red coats, but very modern. Examine the knowledge of rules and procedures. Yell a bit. Give the boys some chewing out. Poor fellows.

I used to go through the same shit when I served my compulsory year in the military, though back then it was in green fatigues, behind a high fence, with no marching band and no watching tourists. Here, they have turned the military grind into a show. They show tourists a few military secrets, drills like marching and making turns. These red-coats do have an interesting way of marching, I have to say. No goose-stepping, no smashing of flat boot-soles against the ground to make a thundering sound, to scare the enemy witless. On the contrary, the movement of legs is somewhat supple, fluid, silent, as if the point is to sneak up on the enemy and surprise him at the last moment. Perhaps, back then, in the time of red coats, soles were expensive and boots had to last a lifetime. Who knows what elements influence the way an army marches.

We're standing some distance from the proceedings, so the sounds are a bit muted. Anyway, my English is not good enough to understand the shouted orders, indeed, to be familiar with English military terminology at all. Surprisingly, I don't need to. The intonation of the sergeant's yelling is so compelling, so absolutely identical with the one I used to hear on Vimperk Barracks' drill grounds, so authentic to the last cadence, that a few times my legs automatically jerk to execute the order. Why is it that I haven't yet forgotten this useless bit of information, why remembering it still occupies who knows how many of my brain cells, is beyond me. Why is it that a sergeants' yelling is identical all over the world, the same on every side of every Iron, or any other, curtain? Why do human beings anywhere in the world so relish yelling orders at their fellow human beings? Why is it just this particular expression of sub-humanity that the world seems to agree on, that, in some absurd sense, unites the world? I don't know and I am not going to think any more about it. After all, I also remember what my superior, a lieutenant colonel, used to yell at me – Don't think! In the military, you don't think! For once, I'm inclined to shout in response: Yes, sir!

Bonneville

Bonneville. The freeway sign indicates this exit. The exiting highway stretches in a straight line to the North, all the way across this white Utah salt plain to the shade of distant grey mountains. It would bring us to the Mecca, the Lhasa, the Vatican, the seventh heaven of automotive enthusiasts, aficionados, crazies. Speed addicts. Here lies the unique, hallowed spot on the earth permeated with sweet smell of high octane gasoline like a church with incense, the place where you can go as fast as you and your foot on a gas pedal like and your engine allows.

But you don't have to go all the way there. Even around here, along the freeway, you can see tracks in the salty lake bed. Why? Was somebody too impatient? Did he train here? Was he lacking time or money to make the trip to Bonneville? Did Bonneville seem too hallowed ground for his car? Did he feel that his 120-mile-per-hour car shouldn't mingle with much faster Corvettes and Shelby Mustangs? Who knows, maybe he was happy enough speeding here as much as he liked with no danger of a cop ticketing him.

I am inclined to believe that, once again, it is American individualism that made those tracks. Someone had to blaze his own trail, even though the perfect one is just a few miles from here. Individualism so individualistic that it is reluctant to join even a collective of soul-mates. If it is what he likes...

I like the idea that anyone can drive to Bonneville, that the place, so famous and so world renowned that it was known even in Czechoslovakia, is accessible to anybody. In a temple everybody is equal. So, the owner of 120-miles-per-hour Camaro may converse with the owner of a 300-miles-per-hour rocket car. On the Bonneville salt flats – a temple of the Gasoline Brotherhood.

Los Angeles Tangent

Driving from Las Vegas to the Pacific, we just touched the outskirts of Los Angeles. I wasn't interested in plunging into the city without knowing what to look for. I mean, which monuments to visit. Most likely I would lose my way and end up in some neighbourhood where I could get hit in the head with a brick. I didn't long to see the Hollywood, either, not being a fan of their recent productions. I've always considered its moniker *Dream Factory* to be an oxymoron. Life dreams must be tailor made to measure, hand crafted by the most personal imagination; they can't be mass-produced in a factory, no matter how smart and imaginative the workers. Mass-produced dreams – what masturbation of the imagination! Only poor souls are satisfied with them. And we are talking about day dreams, dreams in the sense of life goals, desires, and directions. Night dreams are a completely different matter. You can't buy those at any store or market-place, not even over the internet. Only the depths of your mind can supply you with those. And they do, free of charge, whether you like it or not.

What I mean is that I don't need Hollywood as a supplier of my dreams. After all, even in Hollywood you may get hit with a brick in the head - though in this case, luckily, the brick is just metaphorical. Thank you. There's plenty of material for dreaming anywhere you look. I have my own imagination, so I can cut and stitch a dream or two myself. Don't mention this to anybody, the sellers of dreams are quiet about it, but a reservoir of dreams is practically bottomless, endless, inexhaustible. Just about anything one doesn't have and would like to have can be the object of dreaming: from a scoop of ice-cream to the kiss of a girl with a dimple in her cheeks, to climbing Everest, to discovering a new critter, to commanding a big bank account. Whatever it may be, somebody is dreaming about it.

What do the super-rich dream about, I'd like to know, having just about everything? Being able to buy almost anything. Do they dream at all? Maybe they dream about inflating that *almost* as much as possible until it spreads over the whole world like a pancake. Do they dream about being able to eliminate anything they could possibly dream about? Do I need to say more? Only the Lord has everything. Does He dream? None of our business, I think.

Not spending any time in Los Angeles, we were able to reach the coast and Port Hueneme the sooner. We had our fill of looking at the Pacific Ocean. We found a little hotel not far from the beach. We changed into our swim suits and went for a dip in the Pacific. And one of our dreams – a dream of very long standing - came true.

The Land's End

I suppose that Horseshoe might be a common name for a bay or an inlet. I know two of this name. One appears in a children's book by Arthur Ransome, the other may be encountered a few kilometres before Vancouver, as you drive down from Whistler, on the Sky to Sea highway. We found a motel there and right from its window we could see not only this bay of the Pacific, but also the dock for the Vancouver Island ferry. In the skies, over the little harbour full of sailboats and motor boats, we could see cormorants flying. Real, live cormorants. Another first in our lives. The ferry, coming and going, sounded its horn as only a ship can. Romantic calls of far away lands. The romance of leaving for unknown destinations. Watching cars entering the ferry, made our vague longing focus rather quickly. We had neither time nor money to transport the car and explore Vancouver Island, but we were still attracted to that ship. After all, as children we had enjoyed a few rides on a paddle wheeler on the Vltava river in Prague. Being grown up now, how about taking a ride on a ship so big that it can sail on the Pacific Ocean? Just for the thrill of it! Just whisper to yourself – Pacific... this is *the* Pacific Ocean, dummy... the Pacific Ocean... When will you ever have this same chance again? The temptation grows stronger, the bullhorn call is harder to resist. If we do not resist, we will be able to say – we sailed the Pacific. And, as a bonus, we'll be able to put our feet on the very western end of Canada. Having travelled this far

West, being so close to the westernmost West, should we not make the last step, just to experience the feeling of being on the very edge of the continent?

We board the ferry. Yes, I admit, we're nutty; we lost ourselves to the sound of a ship's horn, pull of far away lands, the call of the West. The ship sounded its horn for us now as well, the water at the stern churned, it parted at bow, and here we go. Of course we spend the whole crossing resisting the winds on the deck. And just like sailing on the paddle-wheeler Vyšehrad at a tender age, this sea-voyage is really full of wonders. You can see the islands, now and then between them you can glimpse the endlessness of the ocean, your eyes can scan the Coastal range of mountains, from the dark grey of the ocean through the green of its slopes to the snowy caps of glaciers to overcast skies. You can see, in the distance, the miniature silhouette of downtown Vancouver. And you can compare what you see with what you remember reading, some forty years earlier, in a book about Captain Vancouver's discoveries.

In Nanaimo we shoot a few photographs at the totem and buy an ice-cream, I mean Nanaimo bar of course. We're heading back, right away, on the same ship. And we see a seal, right in the sea, and couple of killer whales. No point in mentioning seagulls, they can be seen everywhere, but for cormorants you have to come to places like this.

I don't know why, but somehow we needed this trip. Perhaps we needed to add some nautical miles to those we have travelled on land. I think we had to leave our footprints at the westernmost edge of Canada. As if this sea voyage was necessary to round up our travellers' resume.

Exotics

I'm quietly driving along a side-road in south-central Utah, cruise control set at 56 miles per hour. The lush green valley is peaceful and deserted, the highway is empty except for one car approaching from the opposite direction. What do you know, it's a cop. So what, I'm driving within the speed limit. Who can he check when there's no traffic on this road? In my mirror I see him make a U turn. He catches up with me, flashes his lights. What does he want? I haven't violated any traffic rules. I stop.

An older, deliberate, rather fatherly looking guy with a trooper's stetson comes to my window. I was speeding, he claims, his radar indicated 57 miles per hour, two over the limit. He asks for my driver's licence. In a few minutes he's back. He has to issue me a warning, I was driving only a bit too fast, after all. He's almost apologetic. What brings us to his beat? Where are we heading? We have a nice friendly talk, for say, no more than five minutes, then he touches the rim of his stetson with two fingers and I am free to continue driving. He makes another U turn and drives away too.

Jana voices the opinion that he stopped me just because he was curious, having seen our licence plate. Perhaps, in rural Utah, Ontario may be seen as a distant and rather exotic place. This surprises me. This angle of looking at our travelling hasn't occurred to me yet. She's right. I now understand that when I am in distant, highly unfamiliar, exotic lands, automatically, reciprocally, I can be considered an exotic being by the locals. I can be looked at, approached, even studied. It's a strange feeling , this becoming exotic on one's travels.

Crossing Northern Iowa

It's getting darker, we should start looking for a place to camp. We haven't had much experience in the US, it's our first American trip. We could sleep in the van, so that should not be too big a problem, but Iowa doesn't allow overnight roadside parking. Besides, we need the security of a campground. America is said to be a dangerous place. Even in daylight danger lurks everywhere and at night the danger is completely everywhere and then some. From dangerous individuals. Because of the pressures of this ever-present danger the cops are touchy, too, rather trigger-and-truncheon happy. At least this was what the Czech media told us again and again and again. And again. On high alert, we drove through a couple of towns. After all, we'd seen some pick-up trucks with guns in the racks across the back window. No campground in sight, or on the map. All we can see around us is wheat and corn and corn and wheat. We have to keep going. It's getting darker and darker. If we have to pay for a motel, we'll miss that money later on our trip, since we're travelling on a shoestring budget. The gas is running low, so we have to stop in the next town – it might be Osage or Hanontown – I'm not sure, to get some.

It has to happen to us! At the gas station a police cruiser is parked. Perhaps we would be safer while getting the gas and won't get ripped off. On the other hand, they will probably ask for ID. We haven't been asked to pay beforehand. Having filled her up, I enter the store. The cop, an affable looking middle aged man, leans against the counter on which he has placed his stetson. His right hand does not rest on the handle of his colt, but is holding a cup of coffee while the left helps give shape to his story-telling. Two neighbours, each with a beer can in their hand are laughing, as is the clerk behind the counter. They don't look like a group of people concerned that they could be ambushed by criminals at any moment. They look like they're feeling very safe. The cop welcomes us with a friendly "Howdy folks". Will we have a cup of coffee with them? Where are we heading? There's no chance of finding a campground within his beat, it's all farming land, no tourism around here, we'd have to drive all the way past Estherville, where he heard that there might be a campground at some lake.

After finishing our talk and emptying our coffee cups, we continue driving. Our tanks must have been filled with something more than just gas and coffee, because now we're relaxed, we're noticing that parked cars have open windows, that houses are wide open too, with children's bikes on the front lawns, nobody suspect or drunk to be seen, no shooting heard. Simply put, none of these towns looks like a fortress under siege by criminals. On the contrary, they all look quiet and peaceful and safe. Is it because of those guns in pick ups? Or because in those towns the church is still dominant?

I don't know. The fact is that we never did find a campground. In the end we parked somewhere on the outskirts of Estherville. There was some sort of water edge nearby and we could see outlines of some campers. Only in the morning light did we discover that we had parked our van among campers for sale on a dealer's lot. Despite that, nobody came to ask for ID, kick us out, rob us or even shoot us. I think I like north Iowa.

City Lights

Not too far from Alcatraz, maybe two miles as the crow flies, if it flies in a southerly direction, first across the sea, then a bit uphill and downhill again, you can find another monument to extreme individualism and social rebellion. True, it is visited by fewer people than the jail, though, in a sense, it is a monument to the people who tried to figure out how to break through certain other kinds of bars.

Walking up Columbus Avenue, you will find a bookstore, a famous bookstore, and that means a lot, because bookstores very rarely become famous. City Lights bookstore is its name. If I hadn't known it was there, if I hadn't been looking for it, I might have missed it. I've known about it because its fame had reached even Prague in the sixties; the bookstore of Beatnik authors. The publishing house of Beatnik authors. Having read about it, I imagined a bigger, more modern, more spacious, if not outright monumental store. I find a store that's inconspicuous, old fashioned, with the atmosphere of by-gone times, especially in contrast with superstores like Chapters or Barnes and Noble. Small, but highly selective. Unlike Chapters, there are no carpets; the floors and stairs are squeaky. No ambient elevator music. From the upper floor you can see laundry billowing on a clothesline on the neighbouring flat roof. None of this matters; the smaller size is compensated for by greatness of spirit, or better spirits, materialized in the books displaying their spines on the long shelves. When you think about it – it's an interesting contrast – here are prophets of the modern and rebels against the old set in a shop from by-gone times.

Both the shop and the publishing house were established by poet Lawrence Ferlinghetti in the early fifties when the beat generation sought their place in the literary sun. Both still exist and prosper under his management. I like Ferlinghetti's poetry. I can understand why he established his publishing house and how he runs it artistically. What boggles my mind is the question of where his business acumen came from, how he manages to harmonize his poetic talents with the mundane tasks of running the business. Does he hang his laurel wreath on a stand after finishing writing a poem, exchanging it for the green visor of an accountant when he does his books for couple of hours? Does he use different coloured inks for those different tasks? Does he write poetry with the left side of his brain while the right is arranging books on the shelves? Just kidding...

When I was reading about this bookstore in Prague, I could not but be silently envious, not only about the books that readers could buy here but also about the fact that the shop became a magnet for like-minded people, the place where they could meet, get to know each other, hold discussions, participate in this market of inspiration, and through all this could stimulate their growth as artists and people. Descending the squeaky steps into the basement I can imagine the atmosphere of readings, the beehive of poets and would-be poets and fans of poetry and readers and visitors – well, if I had to localize the Beat movement, it would be right here. At least for me. Kind of a Statue of Liberty on the west coast. Of course, this one is not wearing a flowing gown but rather a slightly worn T-shirt and blue jeans, sandals on her feet. In one palm she may be hiding a joint but the other one raises high a book – not the Book of any particular ism; book as such.

Why should this store be such a monument of a rebellion? For one thing, the Beats were social rebels. Not liking America of their day, they wanted her to be somehow different; there was a bit of the anarchist strain in them. And the second and more important reason: every poet, every creator is a rebel. Every new poem, every new paragraph in prose, is an act of rebellion that challenges all that's been written before; it shouts at the literary past: go get stuffed you dinosaurs, I can do it better, more originally. Of course, you might have heard such bragging since the days of Gilgamesh and Homer. Every poet of every generation, chewing his quill in creative agony, rebels, again and again, against the whole history of literature. Some successfully, some less so. The successful young rebel runs into a surprise anyway, since winning his rebellion makes him part of the establishment, and, in his mature years, he finds that it is his works that are becoming disregarded, disrespected, even ridiculed – yes, the former rebel is rebelled against.

Anyway, when favourable stars afford a few poets the opportunity to coalesce into a group, they can, figuratively speaking, share a joint of inspiration, encourage each other, pat each other on back. And when they find an independent publisher who's their colleague and soul-mate, why, they can sneer at the establishment even more, they can afford to be in their writings even more rebellious, wilder, more free. Easy to rebel, then. Is it any wonder that one tends to be envious, looking at it all from from Prague, through the bars of the Iron curtain?

This bookstore is full of rebels, from basement to roof. The inventory seems to reflect the taste and interests of Ferlinghetti and the beat generation. Modern French poetry, Celine, surrealists, Buddhism, Existentialism next to Marxism, all together creating quite a surrealist mixture. I wouldn't be surprised to find a book titled Zen-Marxism here. Yes, it rubs me the wrong way to see here the work of the far left radicals who dedicated their lives to preaching and thundering against the spirit of bookstores like City Lights, but they are more than balanced by works of the true rebels of spirit and imagination that you can't find in any other American bookstore. Well, when they can co-exist on the shelves of the same shop, I should at least tolerate them in my mind. One has to accept the face of the Statue of Liberty as well as her back side.

Fraction of Rivers

Crossing the border between Wisconsin and Minnesota, you drive over a bridge. There's a sign: Mississippi River. You stop on the lookout past the bridge. What? *The* Mississippi? Is this river, running fast at the bottom of this narrow valley, supposed to be the majestic Old Man River? It doesn't looks much bigger than Sázava River in Bohemia.

On second thought, yes, it is the Mississippi, but in the upper course, with which it is never identified, as if it had no upper course, as if it welled up, in full size, from the prairie just before it reaches Saint Louis. The fact that rivers are identified with just a part of their course, is often their fate. Colorado River is reduced to the stream running at the base of The Grand Canyon. As if it hasn't existed before reaching the Canyon and disappears again once it has powered the Hoover Dam. And yet I've seen it winding its way across half of Colorado where it seemed to be a lively, swift and wild, picturesque river, where you can go whitewater rafting. Similarly, the Rio Grande of US and Mexico border fame. Where I wetted my feet in it, not far from Monte Vista in southern Colorado, it was a giddy mountain river jumping from boulder to boulder. A nice river, to be sure, but Grande? On the other hand, the Hudson river, if you can recall where it runs, is just the part that washes Manhattan. We could go pretty much all over America like this. It seems we're nor accustomed to looking at things in their full extent, from source to estuary. And it seems as though we don't care.

Street Performers

Waiting for a ferry to the island where the Statue of Liberty stands, we've had plenty of time to watch performances of one individual and two small groups of street performers. I know, they are all over Manhattan. This one blows a trumpet, that one does a pantomime, another does something with a marionette. Most seem to favour musical instruments. When I ran into them for the first time, I was uncomfortable watching them, even walking past them, because I saw their performances as a sort of thinly disguised panhandling. If they had something real to offer, they would be engaged somewhere and wouldn't need to do a sidewalk show. But pretty soon I was hearing that the one with the trumpet, say, across the street from the Trump tower, was damn good, so good he could be a star with any jazz orchestra in Prague. The mime I am enjoying on this quay is no slouch either. Watching him move to his buddy's saxophone variations, I can feel that both are having fun with their performance. I'm starting to agree with them. I was wrong, this is not disguised panhandling. This is serious work going on. The only unusual specific is that these guys are self-employed and their stage is beneath the blue skies. At times, I even feel that they perform more for the fun, for showing off, for the joy of entertaining people, than for those few bucks they collect in their hat. So they go to perform where people gather rather than trying to entice people to come for a performance. Why, then, should they seek some steady engagement, representation by some agent, the supervision of a principal or impresario?

What I saw in New York streets is a direct descendant of vaudeville, outdoor vaudeville. And of a much older tradition as well, vaudeville's great great and so on forefather - market performances. Here I am, folks. Stay for a moment. Open your eyes and ears and hearts, evaluate me. If I entertain you – here's my hat. If I don't – you can keep going. Tightrope walkers, clowns, artists, dancers, musicians, story-tellers of some antique agora or forum... Art in its protoplasmic, primeval phase, the stem cells that, over the centuries, branched out and developed into contemporary artistic forms... repeats itself on the sidewalks of New York at the end of the twentieth century. Small -a- art, art without publicity, media, critics, reputations, million dollar investments, taxes, without all that humbug called show business. Art relying on direct contact, direct feedback. Folks on the sidewalk, relaying on their own eyes and ears and minds, have a look and then give the thumbs up or thumbs down. Good. Keep on working at becoming good.

I find it interesting that this artistic undergrowth, this hotbed, is most active in New York, the city with arguably the best organized and most complex show business in the World. Maybe that's why. But I think it's mostly because all these artists have freedom to just roll out their mat on the sidewalk and offer their artistry to the passing public.

Aboard the Ferry

I wonder what kind of impact commuting to work every day via a ferry, instead of driving or taking a subway might have on one's mind. Sailing daily across San Francisco bay, say, from St. Raphael to the city itself. Most of the commuters look indifferent, even bored. Some read a newspaper, some a paperback thriller, presumably to get their daily dose of excitement. They have no idea that plenty of dramatic vistas roll in front of the passenger standing outside the cabin, at the rail of the deck. His mind is giddy with anticipation. He's finally going to see with his own eyes the city he heard and read so much about, first in Bohemia and then in Canada. Of course, he knows that reality may diverge from expectations.

He's sailing past San Quentin prison. He's familiar with the name, but didn't know it was here, so close to the city. He sees a few small islands and the Golden Gate Bridge in the background, with other bridges spanning the whole width of the bay, super-structures attesting to the large scale symbiosis of imagination, engineering and mathematics. In the distance, he sees the Rock also called Alcatraz. He's surprised how big the bay is, though he can see only a small part of it. When he read a Jack London biography, many years ago, he was puzzled about how youngster Jack could be an oyster pirate in this bay, how he could get away with it, keep it secret. Of course, back then, in Prague, he imagined a bay on the European scale, having no idea about the size and ruggedness of the San Francisco Bay. He couldn't imagine that it could easily hide the whole Pacific fleet, let alone the tiny sailboat of a thieving teenager. Seeing the panorama of San Francisco itself, he's surprised that it opens towards the bay and not the Pacific, as he expected on the basis of his reading. He's also surprised that it dares to have any skyscrapers at all, considering that it lies directly on the San Andrea fault. Well, all those misconceptions are common, inevitable, in a reader who projects what he's reading about on the screen of his experience.

The paperback thriller reader has no idea that the mind of the passenger at the rail is rocked by conflicting information, air-raided by a squadron of question marks. What kind of city is San Francisco? Its reputation for extraordinary tolerance has always attracted eccentrics and oddballs and fallen angels of all kinds, people who have had trouble fitting into the moral corset of mainstream America, rejects from other parts of the country, from Alcatraz inmates, say, to disgraced politicos and businessmen, to beatniks and hippies, to inventors of perpetuum mobile, to thinkers attempting the synthesis of Judaism with Islam, colourful dubious characters convinced of their own genius, not to mention dozens and dozens of messiahs and prophets of any conceivable cause under the sun. The latter have a good chance of finding followers and succeeding here, as San Francisco has been a city capable of absorbing any rebellion, digesting it and adopting it as the mainstream, all within a decade. The downside of this tolerance is the fact that prophets have been running out of available causes, becoming rebels-in-search-of-a-cause.

San Francisco is the city where right behind a church is a red-light district and within that you can find a brand new school, its gates facing a porn cinema, presumably to make education and life go hand in hand, the city with plenty of magnificent flowers blooming everywhere, the city containing garages where the giants of computer business have been established, and also the garages and galleries where good poetry has been read. The city boasting the crookedest street in the world, the street so steep that its roadway has to zigzag down in a serpentine manner and its sidewalks have to be side-stair-walks. Tourists, passing by, pause there to watch cars testing their courage, inching their way down, brakes smoking, their white knuckled and eyes-popping drivers mumbling prayers to increase the chances of stopping at the stop sign midway down there. If they succeed, they throw a triumphant look at the onlookers and keep going; if not, they turn right or left pretending that was their intention from the very beginning. The street is rightfully almost one of the symbols of San Francisco and its metaphor as well; a wild ride swaying from one curb to another, steeper and steeper, faster and faster, until the ride becomes unstoppable and the driver has to pretend it's normal, exactly what he intended. It is a city that has its own visual face, since it is architecturally different from the rest of America, a city that, in spite of the faith of its patron saint, seems to worship anarchy more than anything else, a city that, in its own way, represents American freedom pushed to the extreme. In short, next to New York, it's the city with the most personality – for better or worse. How might all these contradictions influence the inhabitants, their minds, their thinking? The traveller wonders.

The ferry slows down, a few more metres to the pier, the commuter closes his thriller and starts his routine walk to some office to do his boring job, while the tourist heads into the city to look for some answers to his questions.

Mount Rushmore

Homo Pragensis, that is the citizen of Prague, even a former one, is touchy when it comes to mega-monuments. He still remembers very well the monstrous mass of generalissimo Stalin's monument, situated on the promontory over Vltava river, so placed that you could see it pretty much from the whole of Prague. The grey concrete of the mega monument was so mega heavy that the whole hill started to slide and collapse under it. Of course, the statue was built to survive eternity, or at least to last longer than the Egyptian pyramids. The pyramids did not have to fear its competition. Eternity proved to be rather temporary, even short-term. The monument lasted about ten years. Then the great mega Leader with the concrete heart was blasted to eternity with dynamite. We were fifteen years old then. History was rewritten, the greatissimo marshallissimo generalissimo ceased to be the *pinnacle of the cone of which the Universe is the base,* as poet Christian Morgenstern might have described him. For us teenagers that dynamite blasted to smithereens and forever scattered the conviction that anything in history and society was constant and unchangeable. Everything can be dynamited out, rewritten. A saint can be stripped of his sainthood, a giant re-sculpted into a gnome.

Fortified with this experience, is it any wonder that in the Black Hills of South Dakota I sought Deadwood rather than

Mount Rushmore? Still, there was plenty of time left after Deadwood, the monument was not that far away, and, after all, it is one of the pilgrimages in America, so we decided to go. I was pleasantly surprised. The trails to the lookout were decently made and done more as a tribute to America than to any individual.

Many things run through my mind on the lookout terrace. The first thing is that the sculptors of Stalin's monument must have been driven crazy by the awareness that no matter how big they made their megalomaniac idol, it would still be dwarfed by those heads there. Second, here they used dynamite for building, not destroying. But still, why should this monument become an object of pilgrimage, a national monument? It attracts quite a few people even though the Black Hills are a bit out of the way. Sure, it's a celebration of US history, of the USA, but I tend to believe that beneath this admiration, even adoration, rests one of the oldest archetypes – that of the old Prometheus, chained to the mountain as if it were a monument to himself, a monument to his courage to defy the gods, to his Titanism. That's what runs through my mind when I look at the four likenesses chiseled from the mountain face. Just like Prometheus, they rebelled against the gods of their days, refused to accept the ruling conditions as divinely decreed and immutable, and started changing them, reshaping them, replacing them with their own. They brought people the gift of freedom. A rebellion worthy of Titans. Worthy of a monument. Worthy of a visit. Titanism is a quality that attracts people of all ages.

Encounter Among the Remainder Books

Returning north from DisneyWorld, just past the Florida borders, take the very first freeway exit in Georgia to a big bookstore that sells remaindered books, leftovers that couldn't be sold in a regular bookstore. The last refuge of books, their last chance of finding readers. The store sells them very cheap, almost for a song. When I see the sign for a remainders bookstore, I can't keep driving as if I had seen nothing. I spent among the high shelves full of books, just like in some library, quite a bit of... well, let's say we might have been somewhere close to Atlanta by the time I emerged.

Quite unexpectedly, I ran into my own past. I mean to say, I ran into somebody I used to know. It's always pleasant to find a book of your countryman elsewhere in the world. It's doubly pleasant if he happens to be a fellow emigrant. The rarest and most unusual pleasure comes when you knew him in Prague. As I used to know poet Jiří Gruša. The English translation of his novel *The Questionnaire* smiled at me from the shelf. Taking the book in my fingers triggered a chain of memories.

I used to know Mr. Gruša, not particularly well, but for some ten years. Then, in 1978, I read this novel in *samizdat*, a sort of underground publishing, illegal, but at the time the only way to read good literature in Bohemia. It meant reading the novel in seventh or eighth carbon copy, overnight, because the next reader was anxiously waiting his turn. If I wanted to have a copy in my own library, I would have to type the whole novel, keep one or two copies and send the rest to circulate. If I were able to hold up the circulation of the manuscript for two weeks or so, I might have undergone the copying; it would have been neither the first nor the only book I acquired in this manner. I fell in love with this novel. I was amazed not only by its content, imagination and poetics, but also by its pristine Czech language. Of course, I knew about the author's passion for the language. About a year earlier I had asked him to have a look at my attempts to write poetry. He blasted to nothingness over ninety percent of it, could live with five percent and recognized as passable poetry the remaining two or three percent. During that healthy massacre of my outpourings, he gave me some advice about writing, advice so sound that I could build on it for a number of years and you may find some applications of it even in this book. That was our last meeting. Though *The Questionnaire* was not a political book, the authorities found it cheeky, subversive and criminal. Gruša spent a few weeks in jail, then was stripped of his citizenship and exiled, against his will, to West Germany. He later became a respected German poet and essayist.

Now, of all places, I run into him in this last refuge of books in an insignificant town in Georgia. It took fifteen years of living in Canada to see in the full light the absurdity of the Czechoslovak cultural situation back then. Just imagine: a small group of comrades who might have been literate, but were certainly literarily uncouth, decided what literature was and was not, applied purely political criteria to decree what would get published and what wouldn't, who would qualify as a poet and who wouldn't, whose brow would be decorated with laurels for services to the regime and who would be thrown into jail for writing real poetry. They even had the power to excommunicate and exile the poet from his native tongue and literature. Which left readers like me without a chance to be influenced and inspired by good writing.

Closing the bookstore door with this treasure in hand, I couldn't but say to myself: Praise the Lord that for the last several years I could be living in the more reasonable half of the world and of publishing. Finally I would be able to read Gruša in depth, take my time to analyze his poetics, without having to type the whole novel. Though, truth be told, the shadow of totalitarian absurdity was a long one, reaching over all of fifteen years, all the way to Georgia, USA. There used to be times when I would give a lot for having this book, for the possibility of opening up to its influence. Since I couldn't have it, since it was not available, it was priceless. Today, when its inspirational power for me must have dissipated to some degree, I can buy it for $1.90. I had been charmed by the beauty of its Czech language – I would enjoy it in English. Better late than never, better in English than not at all. I was glad that this work had wandered so far away from Bohemia. After all, when it comes to literature, true poets are inhabiting a surprisingly small world.

In Canadian Utah

Canada is so big that you can find almost the whole world within her borders. And not only in terms of population. As expected, you can find a piece of France in Quebec, a bit of Finland in Northern Ontario, Ukrainian steppes around Vegreville in Alberta, an Austrian mountain village in Sun Peaks and a Bavarian village in Kimberley, not to mention chinatowns here and there.

There is a piece of Utah southwest of Kamloops in British Columbia, along highway number one towards Lillooet. A strangely charming landscape, dry and treeless, where around some waterhole you might find a few bushes, but mostly stones and rocks - not as wild and red as in real Utah. Short, sun-burnt grass gives the landscape a yellow-brownish hue. It's neither mountain, nor prairie. Perhaps an undulating high plateau. Whatever it is is not without charm.

We didn't expect to find much tourism in this kind of land, nor a good campground. We hoped to drive through it to reach a more camping-friendly area before dusk. Still, there was a sign for a campground which we found about a kilometre from the highway, at the bottom of a huge dale, in almost a half crater, washed out over millennia by the fast running Thompson river. The campground didn't look bad. Even a cluster of pine trees grew there from white sand.

Nobody was in the camp office, though the light was on, the door open, a stack of registration forms and a pen provided. There was a cardboard sign on the counter: *Gone fishing. Help yourself. Coffee is ready.* The sign bore signs of frequent use. Somebody must be fishing often. Why not, the river runs maybe twenty steps away. I filled in the registration card and left ten bucks on the counter. I had no doubts that both would stay there, especially in house with an open door. I had lived in Canada long enough for such trust.

We found our spot on the river bank, cleaned out some river-rounded stones and erected the tent. Tonight we would sleep comfortably, on soft, beach like sand. We had just finished our dinner when a somewhat wild looking woman stampeded toward us. Though in the firelight she looked about eighty, she was as energetic as a twenty year old. Rubber boots, shorts, T'-shirt, pipe in her mouth, stetson. Fishing rod in one hand, a fish in the other, as fresh as possible, guaranteed, still wet. She had caught it for us. For our dinner. She was very, very sad to hear that we had already eaten. Her freezer has been packed with fish long time ago and if she wants to keep on fishing, she has to give away her catch. There's wonderful fishing in this river. She's fishing on request, so to speak. As soon as she sees a car turning on the road to the campground, she grabs her rod and runs to the river. In most cases she gets her fish before the guests have put up their tents or settled their RV. She tried to talk us into having a second dinner. Luckily, for us and her, another guest then made it to the campground and hadn't had their dinner. Long into the night we heard her entertaining them at their campfire. Her youthfully exuberant voice was reaching our tent somewhat muted by the distance, as if she were half-whispering us bed-time stories. Fishing stories. She had a lot of them.

Rebellion in North Dakota

You find no indication of it when you cross the border from Montana, though, as usual, you can feel some difference. Have you noticed? The landscape is the same on both sides of the border, and yet each side gives you a slightly different feeling, a different ambiance. I don't know why. Perhaps it has to do with the euphony of the state name or some such subconscious influence. Here, in westernmost North Dakota, you first wind your way through Badlands, then the landscape improves until the land becomes good and the Interstate straightens up.

The asphalt surface is of excellent quality with no cracks or even minor potholes. Not a single reflective lane marker is missing, nor is there any peeling off the milestones. All the freeway signs look as if they were just installed. Something doesn't look quite right in the surrounding fields though, and then you realize that cubes of straw, disgorged by combines, are precisely aligned in both axes. The same goes for rolls of hay. The impression is of a straw army. The farmer must be a retired drill sergeant. Then you realize that his neighbours must be ex-officers too, or at least adherents of military discipline. The cows in one herd are all the same colour – as if in uniform - and graze with their heads all in the same direction. The farms are all right angles and squares, no peeling paint, no imperfection whatsoever. Hedges are cut as if along the trajectory of bullet. Even the gathering storm clouds look like as if they strive to assume the form of cubes. We pass a state trooper's car on the shoulder. We slow down a bit, to the speed limit – exactly the speed limit. We don't doubt that he would give us a ticket if we exceeded the limit by 0.67 miles per hour in this neighbourhood. I am sure he knows and follows his rules and operating procedures to the last dot on the I and cross on the T. This local, how to put it, neatness, precision, is not unpleasant; it just feels somewhat unAmerican. That is, it's American and unAmerican at the same time, because accepting the unAmerican is a feature of America. Oh yes, now I understand, the capital of North Dakota is Bismarck. That's the answer. The spirit of the Iron Chancellor hovers over the local fields and waters. All is efficient, accurate, rational, organized, ordered.

Also Halt! I mean Stop! Stop it, man! You can't do this, can't make stupid fun of the honest people who live here. You may not be stupid in general, but now you are acting like an idiot. Forget for a moment about Czech conditioned reflexes, they are adopted anyway, and think for yourself. What is required to make people laugh? Right, a shared background. Do you share that in this particular case? Right, you don't. Making fun of the military is a Czech characteristics because in Czechoslovakia every young male had to serve for two years in uniform and the officers corps were a bunch of arrogant and cruel idiots. One's helplessness against their chicanery and bullying was truly unforgettable producing lifelong hatred of or at least contempt for anything military. The only way to ventilate and lighten up such frustration was irony and humour. It doesn't work here. This army is professional. High quality. A military career is respected and esteemed. So in this context your fun-making is hard to understand and, of course, unamusing. It might even be offensive. So shut up. It's the same problem with things German. German jokes work in Bohemia thanks to centuries of conflict with the neighbouring German element. They might work somewhat in the rest of Europe, owing to WWII, but they don't work in North Dakota. Because of your inherited way of thinking, you may dislike some features associated with the German psyche, but there's no need to ridicule them en bloc.

Have another look around. What kind of living does the state offer? Pleasant, comfortable, I would say. Isn't striving for perfection a positive thing, after all, allowing for a quiet, peaceful life? Isn't German efficiency and industry the reason why the state is so affluent? The reason why a good steak dinner costs about half of what it would elsewhere and a cup of coffee costs a nickel while at the neighbours it costs fifty cents? True, lots of things are predictable here, but on the other hand citizens can do without bars on their shops and feel safe in the streets at night. Bismarck probably offers better living conditions than New York or San Francisco. Is there any room here for un-conventionality, for improvisation, imagination? Sure there is, we are still in America. The rigidity I have described is more a tendency than an ironclad rule. And I can prove that with our camping experience tonight.

Nobody was camping in the campground on the town's outskirts. Nobody was in the office, though the coffee maker gurgled there. Nobody answered my call. Only the cuckoo clock on the wall kept ticking. The ticking silence felt weird, like a scene from some Hitchcock movie. The showers and toilets were spotless. No people anywhere. We couldn't register, we would have to stay here as some wildcatters, anarchists. The office remained empty. Overnight, then in the morning. I began to like the situation. I hoped that the person who was absent from the office, was missing not because he had to be, but because he wanted to be. Because he preferred to be with his girlfriend, for example. When we were leaving in the morning, I left ten bucks on the office counter. The coffee was still gurgling. To my ears, its rhythm sounded like a military march. I couldn't help that, but I smiled inwardly and didn't hold anything against it.

Roaring Fork

What a beautiful name! Do you like it as much as I do? According to my map, there's more than one Roaring Fork, the best known being the river and valley around Aspen in Colorado. I have in mind another one, probably just a local name in southern Colorado, on the way from Cortez and Dolores over San Juan National Forest to Telluride. Roaring Forks Creek. We have a weakness for interesting names and a soft spot for camping outside official campgrounds. We like entering roads that lead somewhere but don't make it all the way there, expiring along the way, becoming dead ends. We like places where few people go.

The dirt road with this beautiful name, probably an old lumber road, follows the flank of a ridge in a narrow valley with a wild stream skipping at its bottom. In some places it is damaged by minor landslides, so you have to drive carefully, close to the other rocky side, ascending not steeply but steadily. After fifteen or so kilometres, the road crosses the stream and swings to the other flank in a wide turn, three times wider than necessary. Plenty of room to park our van there, to set up our camp for the night. Off the road and on the road at the same time. The wild river with its potable water gurgles just a few steps away. Plenty of dry firewood everywhere. No picnic table but a nice thick log that can be rolled to the fireplace to serve as a bench to sit on. Yes, this is our way of camping. There is nobody within fifteen kilometres, nobody to prattle, shout, play his radio, or shoot his gun as in that campground in Vail.

We love being alone with the waning light of dusk, the smell of spruces and firs, stones, the bubbling of the river, the whispering of aspen leaves, the crackling of the flickering fire. Nothing stands between you and your imagination, nothing prevents you from *not* seeing your parked van and believing that your horse is grazing the tiny meadow on the riverbank, your Winchester within your reach. You'll have a pan of beans and bacon for dinner and your coffee will be brewed in a tin kettle over the fire and drunk from a tin cup. The darkness dissolves the time; it could be the year 2000, or, just as easily, 1880 or 1850. When you descend the few steps to the stream to wash your greasy pan in the morning, you're almost certainly going to find some gold dust in the sand. If you venture deeper into the forest and stay quiet, you will see how much alive it is.

This bend in the road offers such a natural diffusion, a blending together of the present with a boy's dreams. Just as it was so many years ago before falling asleep, it's up to your imagination where it will carry you, the only difference being that you're not huddled in your comforters in Chotouň but sitting on a log on a dirt road, under the stars of Colorado; you've already seen a decent bit of America and you know how things look around here, so now your imagination can offer you more specific images, more realistic backdrops. To tell the truth, by now you're dreaming much less, almost not at all; the stream of images running through your mind now reflects more the places you have already seen, recalling, remembering your rich experience. As you feed the fire with fresh sticks, you quietly, unhurriedly, sort out the contents of your memory, organizing your experiences like a boy sorting out his postage stamps and putting them in his album. Your memory's getting clearer through this process, so that in the morning, waking with the first sun, your mind will be clear and crisp, ready to charge back into civilization again and absorb new experience. While this fork may be roaring in name, in reality it offers the pilgrim a moment of stillness and silence.

Oregon Trail

If my Dad, in writing his lyrics, had in mind a real journey across the prairies and not an emigration, the best way to gauge how long that journey would be, would be to follow the Oregon trail. Not the whole length. As a sample, to give him some idea, it would be sufficient to travel across Nebraska. Even these days, to cross Nebraska, the five hundred miles from Omaha to the Wyoming border, seems almost endless. Add to it the whole width of Wyoming and you would still be only about half way to your destination – Oregon.

It must have seem a great deal longer back then. A horse or oxen team pulled a covered wagon carrying your whole property. You were walking alongside. The whole way. How much per day? Twenty, thirty kilometres? For how long could the travellers see Chimney Rock, as a lighthouse in the prairie, before they reached it, and how long before it disappeared bellow the horizon again? Travellers had to average those thirty kilometres a day to make the journey in one season. They had about six months, from the start in Saint Louis, to reach the Rocky Mountains, cross them, and then trek across the whole of Oregon to the Pacific coast. Some 3200 km. If they reached the Rockies too close to the first snow to cross them safely, they had to build a sod-house to survive the winter in Wyoming. I saw such a dwelling in the South Dakota Badlands, and I can tell you that it's better than a tent or nothing, but I would still be very reluctant to spend a winter in it.

Of course, even back then, it was very helpful being in America. The trail was blazed by the travellers themselves and not designed and staked out by surveyors and some planning committee, so it followed their needs; it was so well set up and practical that even the modern freeway still follows the same route. Across the prairies, the trail sought the greenest areas with grazing for the horses, never venturing too far from the river to be near water, never having to go too much uphill or downhill to avoid getting stuck and having to push the wagons. Of course, given the entrepreneurship of the American people, businesses were springing up along the trail: blacksmith shops to shoe the horses and cobblers to re-sole boots, dealerships with fresh "horses" of all makes, general stores with everything from flour and bacon to ammo and matches, not to mention shops to repair everything that could get broken, saloons, and, presumably, graveyards. The proof that those services were located in the right spots is in that they still exist, having grown into today's towns and cities. The railway follows the same trail. Anyway, when I imagine what such a journey must have entailed and demanded, I tip my hat very, very low. Truth be told, we've had pretty tough forefathers and foremothers. Compared to theirs, our immigration was an easy walk.

How much of this did my Dad know? How long did he imagine the whole journey to be? He must have been thinking in the European scale of distances. I don't think he could have realized that the trail was much longer than from Prague to the very end of the European continent in Portugal. I don't know, I will never know. But I am sure that this journey to the West took much longer than my Dad *could* ever have imagined. Nor could he know that when you succeed in making it to the end of the trail, relieved that your hardships are over, you have only reached the real starting point in your immigration journey.

Downside of Being Big

It's difficult to please today's traveller. He's driving around Thunder bay to the West, passing through forests and forests for half a day, for almost the whole day seeing nothing but trees, and he starts grumbling and cursing, claiming that sight of one more tree will drive him around the bend and make him insane. Just before that happens, though, he emerges onto the prairies near Winnipeg. He drives and drives, half a day, almost the whole day, with not a single tree in sight, nothing but flat yellowish grass. In the middle of this flat infinity the traveller feels tiny and insignificant as an ant and starts grumbling and cursing, claiming that unless he sees a small hill or a roll of terrain, he will be driven around the bend. But before he really reaches the snapping point, he rolls into Saskatchewan and his sanity is saved by plenty of rolling and wavy terrain, all around him, and he drives through it for half a day, almost a whole day, and he feels the approach of insanity again, again by the absence of any trees. He's been crossing Alberta and the prairie is still bald, my kingdom for a single big tree, there is none within sight until he enters the foothills of the Rockies and all of a sudden the prairie starts rolling and swelling up so much that all that riding of waves up and down makes him almost sea sick. He sees as many trees as he could wish for, and then some. Now he's driving half a day, almost a whole day, and all of a sudden there are too many mountains and too many trees for him to deal with, making him fearful of claustrophobia, and he feels like he'll go insane if he can't have a bit of flat, treeless prairies soon...

I guess, it's the price we have to pay for Canada being so big, so expansive. We've got everything in Canada, the best of everything, but on such a mammoth scale that even a mammoth would wear off his legs walking from one kind of terrain to the next. The mammoth has long legs and is patient. He has time, certainly in comparison with a modern human. For us, no change is fast enough. That's why we think that the slowly changing landscape in Canada drives us crazy, pushes us to the edge of insanity. Well, the landscape is not to blame. We are, our impatience, the rapid tempo of our lives. It looks like we are not mentally attuned to the size and rhythms of our own landscape. And yet, the Canadian landscape always has mercy on us. Eventually, to our relief, it alters.

Hats

Where did all the hats disappear? I mean men's hats, all those fedoras and homburgs, trilbys and other soft brimmed hats. In the few black and white movies of American proveniance that I had seen other than westerns, all the men wore hats – bad guys, good guys, everybody. Wearing a hat was probably the only thing that good and bad guys could agree on. Humphrey Bogart in a baseball cap? Good gracious! Clark Gable bareheaded and with messy hair? Get outta here! Gary Cooper in a toque? Enough! Half of the stars manly elegance would have been missing. To place the hat on your head in your own personal way, and wear it with some style, was an art of a kind. To appear without a hat moved you, in the eyes of your neighbours, somewhat closer to barbarian status, but if you insisted on running around hatless they could live with that.

In Bohemia, hats were driven to extinction, we could even say murdered, around the time of my childhood, in the fifties. It was decreed that hats were of bourgeois origin and that their wearing would be non-revolutionary, maybe even counter-revolutionary. Cloth flat caps and worker's caps were considered synonymous with the working classes, Russian fur karakul or papakhi, home knit toques, berets, anything but traditional hats. I'm not joking. To such extremes went the ideological zeal of the comrades, such trifles occupied the minds of the architects of the Better Future. I don't know why. Perhaps some important comrade could not wear a hat with style, but more likely wearing one wasn't in the Russian tradition. The campaign against hats was enforced with ridicule, calls onto the carpet, and records in your dossier. That's why I say they were murdered. When I reached adulthood, hats were no longer around.

I run into them in America. Hats have been in retreat here as well, but it has taken much longer to drive them into oblivion. When we came to Canada, in 1983, we would occasionally see somebody sporting a hat. Not often, though. One of the hat-wearers was even on TV, reading the news. With his hat on. It looked out of place. TV is broadcast from a studio, and even my very sketchy awareness of hat etiquette tells me you don't wear a hat indoors.

When we drove into the city of Cody, Wyoming, for the first time, I found a store full of stetsons of all colours. We saw guys wearing stetsons in the streets; some even wore them with a three piece suit, as part of formal-wear. They looked good. I liked the way they looked. I decided to buy a hat, though I didn't intend to wear it, just as a souvenir from Old Faithful. I would hang it on my wall at home. But for the time being I was driving in it and forgot to take it off when we drove into the campground. I entered the camp office wearing it. Only when I returned to the van did I notice that thing covering my head. I shuddered. First - lack of etiquette, I didn't tip my hat. Second – worse, much worse, how had I missed that I was wearing a hat at all, how could I have overlooked that? Strange, none of the seven people in the office looked at me askance, neither derisively or threateningly showing how upset they were by my non-conformity. Nobody remarked in a stage whisper that when I grew up there would be general relief. They all looked like they didn't care, as if going hatted is normal. Maybe it is, here, in the West. Perhaps in the West, every head can wear whatever it wants to, being considered competent enough to decide for itself. And if this is not the case, it must be that people are much more tolerant around here than they were in Bohemia in the days when hats were decreed to be of the wrong class origin and that as symbols of a class enemy they must be discarded on the ash-heap of history.

Athabasca

Athabasca is one of those names you can hear just once and never forget. Even though you were born in Prague. A fascinating name, a detonator of imagination with huge potential, the name conjuring in your mind Indian teepees, whitewater rapids, piles of furs, deep snow, set traps, the echo of wolves howling, long sub-polar nights, birch canoes driven upstream in summer and dogsled teams in winter, frozen waterfalls that become ice-falls, buffalo hunts, blizzards and your steamy breath, northern lights illuminating you chopping wood, huge fur mittens... we've known it all since childhood, we've been there, we've lived through it all while reading... and yet, I somehow never thought about where this river comes from, where it runs before it enters the literary world.

So, while standing, as an adult, at the foot of the Athabasca glacier, someone like me can be easily confused. The map claims that I am standing at the continental divide. I am surprised to find that the divide is not between the Atlantic and the Pacific, as I expected, but involves the Arctic ocean as well. I somehow haven't taken seriously the fact that rivers can also run to the North and empty in the Arctic, probably because on the map it looks like they are running uphill and that seems illogical. The fact, of standing on this divide is just the beginning of the surprises.

Look around. It's the height of summer. Even at this elevation it is quite warm. Despite that, there's ice. Lots of ice. Since time immemorial. Have a closer look at this dirty white flow of ice. It is not a frozen river, water covered with ice; it is a big ice river, a huge stream of ice, immobilized, frozen in time. They say it's very slowly flowing, sliding down through the valley, but the movement is so immeasurably slow, so hard to notice, that for all practical purposes it's been here for ever. At least since the end of the last ice-age, that is some 15000 years and at least the same time during the last ice-age, which makes it around 30,000 years, which, compared with the span of a human life, is as good as eternity. Frozen eternity, its muted time ticking in geological or glacial dimensions.

As it is, however imperceptibly, moving downwards, it reaches a point where its own weight and surrounding temperature trigger a transformation. Wonders start happening. Somewhere around here, underneath my feet, right now, at the bottom of this huge mass of ice, a few crystals start to melt, one ice crystal after another changes into liquid and drops from the glacier. During its short fall, over an inch or five inches of space, before it hits the earth, time accelerates as all the drops slip away from the frozen eternity, enter our time dimension and start ticking in human time, also called four-seasons-time. Those drops of water, freed from the spell of being eternal ice, becoming liquid, are given a voice. They gurgle and bubble and chatter, yielding to the downwards pull of gravity, making rivulets, joining other liberated ice crystals. A few feet away, where the transformation is complete, you can see one or two inches wide trickle in the mud – yes, this is the mighty Athabasca river. In front of your eyes, almost imperceptibly, the eternal voyage of Athabasca as a flow of ice is transformed into the stream of Athabasca as a normal, wet river finding its way down and down and down.

Up here, just liberated from the armour of ice, it pulls up all stops and is wild whitewater splashing all around. Like any teenager, confused and intoxicated by sudden freedom, this youngster of a river is giddy with freedom, loud and unchained, un-chainable, leaping from rock to rock, dancing in eddies, sliding down the rock-faces in waterfalls, taking with it its soft banks. It joins forces with the likes of itself, accepting wild tributaries from right and left, often in the forms of waterfalls. The Athabasca has big picturesque waterfalls not long before it reaches the town of Jasper. Only past that town does the river slow down a bit, meandering through a wide stone-filled riverbed. It will really fill up from bank to bank only when all the winter snows are melting.

I don't know by experience what's further downstream. Haven't been there yet. Only through my books. You can read about this part of Athabasca river too, say in the books about Alexander Mackenzie, before he was knighted. Many years ago, I really enjoyed reading about his voyages of discovery.

Monument Valley

Being familiar with the life story of captain Nemo, with his withdrawal from humankind into the depths of the sea, have you ever thought about how the world above the sea surface must have appeared to him? By coincidence, I had a chance to experience that. One day we started away from the Grand Canyon later than we expected. Before we reached the Navajo reservation straddling the border of Arizona and Utah, it was quite late in the afternoon, and twilight was just a few minutes away. We drove into Monument valley anyway. All around us the twilight started casting its spells, conjuring a somewhat phantasmal world. Three dimensional red-brown towering rocks flattened into two dimensional grey silhouettes. The outlines of this or that mesa, rising from a hardly distinguishable semi-darkness, were taking on clearer and sharper contours against the still light blue skies. Flat top rocks. Table Mountain in miniature. A pedestal for a giant statue. An island rising from the sea bottom. Some larger, some merely right for a single shipwrecked sailor. Craggy monuments and tombstones. Vertical fingers pointing to the emerging constellations. Forget the familiar red-brown-gold colouring of this plain, now everything was in hues of dark blue, various greys and black. Everything was bigger than us, everything was towering above us and made us feel small, insignificant. The progressing darkness dissolved all outlines more and more until they became barely distinguishable, their perception becoming a matter of guessing and sensing. None of it was below us, nor on our level, but squarely above us. An unusual point of view. A bottom view. The view upwards only. We were on the bottom, literally. Yes, we are driving along a former sea bottom and in that semi-darkness it's not difficult to imagine that we're sailing, that our car has turned into a submarine. The dark and fuzzy outlines of mesas and islands above offer a very realistic feeling of observing them from beneath the water. A view of the world from beneath the sea. The view of captain Nemo. The waning light is an excellent illusionist. Because of this light, I haven't seen Monument Valley as it really looks, as most visitors see it. On the other hand, I have been privileged to sail through it with captain Nemo.

Islands and Hydroplanes

Beginnings are hard... There is, as the opposite of not knowing, not one but two kinds of knowing. One is, so to speak, theoretical, the other is deeper, more essential, being a part of your being. Something akin to knowing *about* something and really knowing something. An immigrant has to live in a new country mostly with an old mind. Whatever he brings to the new country is mostly superficial, theoretical, on the level of knowing *about*. For instance, say, you are aware that in Canada some affluent, even rich people live.

Then, on your first vacation, looking for a campground, you see the sign for one, follow a terrible road for five kilometres and finally emerge in a meadow descending to the shores of Georgian Bay of Lake Huron. You look for a place to pitch your tent. It doesn't look possible, since there are lots of cars parked here, the kind of cars that would not befriend your thirteen year old rickety AMC Hornet. New and expensive cars. You make it to the water's edge, to a large combination of boathouse and office. You ask about the possibility of camping. "No problem, Sir. How long would you like to stay? We can rent you a boat, and you can pick an island to pitch your tent on. We rent an island, just for you..." Your fingers subconsciously grab the few scrimped dollars in your pocket; they have to last for the whole ten days and here wouldn't pay for one night. A personal island! Who ever heard of such nonsense! Must be some sort of swindle! You panic and leave. You're scared of the world of big money, feeling that even if you could afford the cost, you wouldn't fit into such a world. Your mistake. Today I know you would be welcomed. And now I'm sorry I didn't ask how much such extravagant fun would cost.

A mere two days later, the situation repeats itself, this time on a lake in the Ottawa River valley. Islands are not for rent here. The meadow on the shore is perfectly trimmed and manicured, decorated with sculpted haystacks. In the parking lot, there are two dozen Jaguars, Mercedes, Audis, BMWs. Not a single tent or camper within sight. Something whispers to you that this might not be the place where you'll be spending the night. On the lake, by the deck, you can see three hydroplanes. The mid-size hotel has a large terrace. Large windows reveal huge crystal chandeliers. Something tells you loudly that this is not where you'll be sleeping tonight. Under those chandeliers and on that terrace, screened against the mosquitoes, some guests are sipping their drinks, looking like they just stepped out of a Scott Fitzgerald party. Long gowns on the ladies, tuxedos on the gentlemen, glasses filled with champagne. Something yells at you that your shorts and T-shirt will not cut it here. You panic, you leave. Without waiting for the butler who has just emerged from the side door. You know what he will politely tell you. After all, you can say the same thing yourself, though in much less polite terms.

Nonsense. Once again, nonsense. It's all in your head. Old thinking. Today, I know that most of those ladies and gentlemen wouldn't mind, wouldn't resent even your shorts. Some of them might stroll down to your tent to strike a conversation, to recall, with some nostalgia, their beginnings with a tent, the days before they made their fortunes. The only real problem was the fact that this was a hotel, not a campground. But you realize all this only after a few years, after some experience of not panicking and running away beforehand.

As I say, those are beginnings...

Canyon to Precambrian

Grey drizzle is saturating the air above an endlessly long, very narrow crack splitting the earth. Torn edges of clouds are obscuring the rim, here and there, of a canyon almost a kilometre deep. Not more than fifty metres wide at this part of the rim. Some sort of stream runs at the bottom. The rocky walls are almost vertical. Almost black. We are told that its oldest rocks are so ancient that they reach back more than two billion years, all the way to the time when this planet was still almost fluid, when proto-continents were about to form and divide and start drifting around, and when, as they sought their place and shape, they sometimes cracked. In addition to being a big crack in the earth's crust, this is a canyon in time. Here, time is not moving forward, doesn't stand still; it is reversing, backing up to the before-anything-was-alive time.

Even the sun's rays are afraid to peek into the canyon, let alone reach its bottom. This is a veritable Tartarus of mythical fame. I think the original entrance to Hades must have been at the bottom of this canyon. It must have been closed down because it was so depressive that even the dead complained about its scariness. Since then, it has served as an emergency escape gate only. When it was still the main entrance, a twin of Kerberos was guarding here, until it died of permanent depression and gloominess. The river at the bottom that from up here looks like a mere brook might be the upper course of Acheron. Alas, they could never get a permanent boatmen here, since Charon asked for a transfer down river, to the main entrance to Hades, claiming that he would go insane here and die of gloom and hopelessness if he had to stay. Nothing alive, nobody, can last too long here. Perhaps Hades himself uses this entrance now and then, when he wants to go out on the town to down a few beers or visit some of his loves, behind Persephone's back. The sad truth is that it is more dead around this backyard of Hades than in Hades itself; in there, you encounter at least shadows or souls or whatever you wish to call them, while nothing ripples the stillness here, not even the echo of birdsong, let alone a bird. You won't find a single fly here, nothing but wallowing scraps of clouds and mist, as if on some Scottish moor in twilight. This Canyon is radiating something so strangely old that even Mummies would go nowhere near it, even if promised eternal life. This Canyon exhales air from the time of molten rocks, before bacteria, before single cell creatures, before anything alive appeared on earth. No sign of anything alive, nothing to animate it, the world of dark shadows, the nook of eternal twilight. Black Canyon of the Gunnison.

Waffle House

Many years ago, reading Steinbeck's *Travels with Charley*, I learned that American English was losing its local and regional characteristics, its dialects. According to the author, it was the influence of national television that was to blame for steamrolling the language into standard issue. He wrote this in the early sixties. English is not my native tongue, so my ear isn't sensitive enough to distinguish minor nuances of speech, but when I drove through Tennessee I didn't need a particularly discriminating ear. In this state, people spoke differently from those in the rest of the US, even from people in the other southern states. There, they were indulging their dialect. Owing to my semi-knowledge of English, now and then I had trouble understanding them. Why it was that they were the only ones who had kept their distinctive way of speaking, I didn't know. Maybe they didn't pay that much attention to to national TV.

They had one other speciality as well. Among the usual assortment of McDonald's, Burger Kings and Kentucky Fried Chicken, now and then you would see a yellow sign spelling Waffle House. Something new for me. What is this? Quite a few parked cars, especially pick ups, always surrounded the establishment. It looked like the place was popular. We tried them for breakfast.

We opened the door and entered... right into the fifties. That is, into the atmosphere of the *American* fifties; if it were the Czech fifties I would still be running. Three sides of a square counter were in the middle of the room, on its fourth side a big stove and kitchen counter provided a workplace for a quickly moving cook. On the outside of the counter were a number of red low stools, not bar-stools, the height of a normal chair. A number of booths with tables lined the outer walls, benches covered with red leatherette, tables topped with Formica or arborite, plenty of lights, even a working jukebox contributing to the good mood with Elvis songs. The guests, mostly men in lumberjack shirts, were eating with obvious gusto. All of it was vaguely familiar from movies, even from Norman Rockwell paintings. For a tourist, and much more so for an immigrant, Waffle House offers a rare, because live, window into the past.

Despite some minor communications problems - the waitress spoke with a strong accent – we succeeded in ordering a traditional breakfast. Sausage, eggs, bacon, toast, pancake. Correction, pancakes, I had several helpings of them. Coffee from a large homely coffee mug, refills going all the time. All that for the prices not that much more than those in the fifties. We liked sitting there though the scraps of conversations from surrounding tables were mostly lost on us. The dialect, you know. What compensated for that was the accent of the local atmosphere. I would call it intensely neighbourly. Old fashioned. The atmosphere of friendly back slapping, of everybody knowing everybody else, and greeting everybody on sight even if you don't know him. Something that is rare to encounter in de-personalized big national chains. I think that though we found them hard to understand, it's good that Tennesseeans don't speak like people on national TV and maintain their local Waffle Houses.

Snapshot in the Kootenays

For many years I used to have certain image lodged in my memory. In Kodachrome. It probably came from some advertising or from a tourist brochure. Maybe even a movie. A little beach of a mountain lake. A gentleman and his lady in bathing suits, knee deep in water. Blue skies. Semi circle of mountains in the background, rocky ones of the alpine kind, with snow on its peaks. In July. Swimming and looking at snow at the same time. The summer snow was important. What an experience, what a joy that must be! Somehow, this conjunction of snow and swimming indicated for me the high life. As if a butler waited right there, just a step out of the picture, holding a silver tray with appropriate tall glasses, ready to open the bottle of champagne stuck in a silver ice bucket resting on the hood of a Bentley convertible. Perhaps the interpretation of this image was influenced by the impossibility of seeing the scene 'live', its inaccessibility, more than by anything else. From Bohemia, any travel to high mountains, the Alps or otherwise, seemed completely impossible. The borders, the Iron curtain and so on.

Cut to some thirty years ahead, the highway from Nelson to Cranbrook in south British Columbia. Right next to the road there's a small beach and a long, a very long lake. The peaks of the Kootenay Range of the Rocky Mountains rise beyond the lake, forming a background. Their peaks are covered with snow.

In July! The sun is hot, the beach is sandy. Three guesses as to what we did. Yes. You got it in one. The water was deliciously cool. We felt like a millionaire family. Multiple millionaire, although no butler, champagne, or Bentley was within sight. I did have in the back pocket of my pants a few hundred bucks, just enough to get us home.

You see, lack of freedom can screw up the optics of your mind; the inaccessibility of something can mislead you. You can be very far from the mark. From the very beginning, this image of mine was about *better society* as usually defined by money. The person who is not free cannot imagine the range of possibilities of the free man, possibilities offered to him by a society that *is* better, but in a quite different sense of the word.

Mystery Spots or New Prague

When I notice a sign *Mystery spot* at the road-side, my hands on the steering wheel remain quiet, my breathing doesn't get any faster, my blood pressure doesn't shoot up. No signal light starts flashing, no turning off the road to follow the sign. More than that – I have to chuckle. For several reasons. Yes, I give the entrepreneur credit that his advertising is a good idea; all he has to do is say *mystery* and your imagination gets going. To lure people with the combination of imagination and curiosity is a very efficient trick. Since the time of Pandora's box and then of Eve's indiscretion with the apple, it's been well known that humankind can not resist being curious. The same examples also tell us that such curiosity can have bad consequences. For me a *Mystery spot* means a barely disguised tourist trap to which I am to be brought by my own imagination, caught on my own curiosity. No way. I don't like the feeling of voluntarily entering any trap. If the fellow had anything of real interest to advertise he would come into the open with it, proud of his wares – the Grand canyon feels no need to hide behind a *Mystery spot* sign, nor does, say, DisneyWorld in Florida. Nor Yellowstone Park, though it offers enough mysteries to keep busy several universities loaded with scientists. Another point – when I'm driving in America, the whole continent is one huge mystery spot for me. Why leave the road then? And the third point – now and then I lose my way, temporarily, landing in a whole pile of mysteries. How come I lost my way? Where am I? How can I get out of here? Where will I end up if I keep driving? The pulse quickens, a mild adrenaline rush is here. Can that be matched with any advertised *Mystery spot*?

So it happened that we exited the I-35 just outside of Minneapolis a bit later than I should have, not realizing I followed the wrong highway until about fifteen kilometres later. We concluded that to come back would be boring. Going ahead might be interesting. Suddenly we saw the sign *Havlíčkovy sady*. Yes, just like that, in Czech, with all the accents. In the middle of Minnesota. Not far down the road was another surprising sign, this time saying New Prague. The mystery of *Havlíčkovy sady* was explained, displaced by the mystery of how the town of New Prague got into Minnesota. I didn't know of its existence. We walked through the town, we had a cup of coffee with traditional Czech pastry. We learned that the population was about half and half of Czech and Swedish origin. How do they get along? There's a long-term grudge on the Bohemian side, because during the thirty years religious war in the seventeenth century the Swedish armies ransacked Prague, carried away a substantial loot of artistic treasures that Sweden is still keeping. I guess that once people immigrate to America they let bygones be bygones.

During our walk we enjoyed several large, hand-painted murals decorating the walls of vacant lots. The former mayor was smiling at us, the voluntary fire brigade rolled out their water pump. For us the most interesting display was a picture of the local Czech brass band from the year 1906, depicting all its members in blue uniforms and with full names written in the Czech manner, complete with accents. All larger than life size. The Henry Rousseau style. If the painting were done on plaster, it might be called a fresco, but this mural seemed to be latex on cinder blocks, so I don't know what to call its technique. But who really cares. The main thing is that the work connected the viewer with the city's history, enlivened a street with its colours, was an homage to the painted individuals and, not least, probably a dream come true for the amateur painter. It was pleasant and warming. You could see that the artist was caressed, if not kissed by Muse.

Pleased and inwardly smiling, we kept on driving; seeing another hand written sign, *Mystery spot,* along the road, we just chuckled. No way. Another artificiality. It is not possible to match the surprise of New Prague, a town that advertises nothing though they have a lot to show. You can't match the interesting places created by ordinary life. Even though... you never know, maybe this time... maybe this Mystery spot hides a UFO airport, Jimmy Hoffa's mausoleum, or the Fountain of Youth.

Original Oranges

From many books, especially travel accounts and biographies, I formed the impression that if you're living in a land where you can just reach out and pick up an orange straight from the tree, you're living as close to paradise as you can get. In Europe, this impression was associated mostly with Spain. Why oranges and not cherries or olives or apricots? I don't know. I suppose this suggestion might be rooted in the fact that for growing oranges you need a warm climate, while most of Europe is closer to shivering than sweating most of the year. In America the image conjures mainly California. True, they grow quite a few oranges in Florida too, but probably the crocodiles there are spoiling the image of paradise. The image of an orange in green leaves is associated with California and contributes to her image as an earthly paradise.

Well, I found out that this paradise image is applicable only to a very small part of that state, valid only in the series of valleys shaped like U, V and W, lying right on the Pacific coast. There you can find palm trees and wild azaleas and colours of everything capable of blossoming. And oranges. Though, even there, the proximity of the ocean makes the air a bit cooler than one expects. But drive just a hundred kilometres away from the ocean, climb up the bare hills to the plateau that stretches over most of California, all the way to the Sierras. You won't see much more than yellow grass around here. Better get a pair of binoculars if you want to see a decent tree. It's way too hot up here; the feeling of paradise has evaporated. Too hot and dry for oranges. Even vegetables can be grown here only with extensive irrigation and watering. It's still good here, this is not the deserts and semi-deserts further south, towards the Mexican border.

Of course, one knows the taste of oranges. Still, the curious will want to make the gesture synonymous with being in paradise, and pluck an orange straight from its branch. You can do that, there are plenty of orange groves along the road, more than enough stands where you can buy fresh oranges by the crate. We bought a big paper bag full. They are softer to the touch than those bought in a store. Their peel feels almost like a tangerine's. The taste, though unmistakably orange, is slightly different, too, a bit more watery, less intense, as if diluted. I suppose the taste gets stronger, more concentrated, when an orange travels in a crate to the market. Having nothing better to do, it is working on becoming as orangy as it can by evaporating some water, thus concentrating the taste.

Sitting in that cooler air, tasting one orange after another, I realized that the case of the oranges might be the same as the case of images of Spain and California. Travellers and pilgrims, telling stories about this or that picturesque, pleasant, corner of the land that had impressed them may have exaggerated a bit. Folk imagination then took this picture-perfect story and ran with it, concentrated it, then applied it to the whole land. That's why, when you personally walk into the land and bite into an orange, or California, you find the reality of this earthly paradise to be somewhat more watery, more diluted than you had imagined.

Sequoias

Take your time staying among sequoias. When you look straight upwards, to their crowns, your head might start spinning, so big and tall are these giants. Better to half sit and half lie in the needles, lean on your elbow, look up, stay still, open your mind. Sooner or later, whether you want to or not, you enter a contemplative mode. Some places, like Grand Canyon, Niagara Falls, or Sequoia National Park, are highly conducive to meditative thinking. They are very inspiring. Somehow, in them you can sense, almost touch, Infinity and, next to it, Eternity. The encounter slows you down, reminds you that no matter how much you rush, how fast you move, you won't get any closer to the end of endlessness in space and time. Touching both metaphysical categories adjusts your standards. Well, sequoias, living monuments of patience, are of this meditation-inducing kind. Maybe it's the smell of their needles that stir up your neurons.

They say the sequoias have been growing here for some three thousand years; they would remember not only Jesus Christ, but even Socrates or Homer, supposing they had made the journey here back then. I think they would have found a very good ambiance for their philosophizing, because of the palpable presence of Eternity. They say, too, that these sequoias are the oldest living organisms on earth. I suppose so. But they have close competition. I have always leaned towards languages as possible winners in this longevity race. They are living organisms as well and Socrates' Greek, say, let alone Homer's, is at least as old as most of the sequoias, maybe older. Languages too germinate and grow and develop and thrive and spread and flourish and proliferate and blossom and luxuriate, surviving just about anything, and, like sequoias, are good at ignoring idiots; they can easily outlast not one but whole dynasties of Asinineuses. Assinine is a god of stupidity I invented.

Language – for a writer it's the same thing as a wand for a wizard, violin for a musician, marble and chisel for a sculptor, breath and molten glass for a glass-blower. The term mother tongue sounds a bit too scientific or bureaucratic to my ears. I prefer the expression Mom's language. I am talking about the language into which we are born and that accompanies us through the whole of life. The language that we learn because we are living it, inside it, through it. This language forms a core around which our whole consciousness crystallizes, to carry us through our whole life. The words act as the building blocks, as bricks of amino-acids that combine into the DNA of our conscience. What is what, how things work, what is good and what is bad, how to live among people. It's kind of the acquired DNA of our social life. Socrates and Homer called it *Logos*, as did the translators of the Bible. Yes, the same Word that was at the beginning of the World and, because of that, at the beginning of the Bible. A word was at the beginning of my consciousness, too, and, without intending to compare, after all, of yours as well, of anybody's, of the collective consciousness. Words, many, many words are inserted through eyes and ears into our minds where they create that lush and thriving and spreading verbal system. It's a microcosmic and simplified model of the big World outside. In the big picture it is common with all other individuals, in details it is just as personal as the DNA.

Languages – other than Mom's. For a writer, they equal a bucking bronco that has to be broken, saddled, domesticated, harnessed, made serviceable. Why? Perhaps because, along with a stream of other words, the notion or slogan, *you are as many times a human being as the number of languages you know*, entered my mind and stayed there. For some reason, some people want to be human more than once. Some succeed. I've met a few idiots to the nth degree, or double assholes. Well, no need to dwell on that. There used to be times in my life when I could speak decent Russian and French, so I suppose I was a multiple human being. I would guess about 2.13 times a person, but maybe that's overly optimistic and the figure is only 1.76 times. Definitely not three times, I didn't know either of those languages well enough to qualify for the whole multiple.

What I mean to say is that, taken literally, the saying is a nonsense. Mom's language is the only one in which you can *be* your whole life, because you learned it by being in it, living it. Other languages, acquired in adulthood, you can only know; they are nothing more than competencies learned rationally, on the basis of the first one. But even though they are just competencies, it's still worthwhile to learn them as each foreign language contains its own world and original perspective, a particular flavor, lightning, personality, craziness. The knowledge of foreign languages enriches because they offer not only a fresh look at Mom's language, but also an insight into foreign cultures and ways of thinking, flashes of unfamiliar optics and criteria. It is amazing that though I have completely forgotten French and couldn't even buy a newspaper any more, I still remember how, say, Villon lived and how magically musical Verlaine sounds in the original. Oddly enough, though you lose the language, you may keep what it brought you. The vehicle of delivery eventually lost its wheels, rusted, disintegrated, vanished, but the delivered load remains. In the case of the Russian load, I'm sometimes tempted to say – unfortunately.

Pardon me, I've been waylaid, distracted. It must be the smell of sequoias, I suppose, causing me to lose sight of my subject. Of course, I'm in the presence of the Infinity of time, Eternity.

The sequoias are materialization of time; looking at them you are looking at three thousand years, their trunks being symbols of continuity from the tiniest roots to the newest little needle in the crown. Of course, you can find the exact parallel in languages, which also have their roots in the dawn mists of pre-history and yet, even if you spoke only Czech or English, you would find that quite a few words, sometimes even sentences – like *the tragic polemic of the Iliad* – would be understandable to old Homer, let alone Socrates. Without realizing it, in speaking we participate in a very old, indeed ancient, ritual. It ties us to hundreds of previous generations. Such lasting power bears the spiritual work of our ancestors.

Of course, if the gods are merciful, or life circumstances force us, we can learn foreign languages quite well. We can absorb some foreign rituals, enrich ourselves with some foreign traditions. But even if we were to become virtuoso in them, it will only be learned virtuosity. We will never have absolute pitch in them. We'll never have the key to their soul. Only childhood confers that.

Language with an accent. Logos with an accent. Paradigms with an accent. It's better than nothing, I should say, as long as you consider knowledge to be a virtue and an asset. Then it is worthwhile making an effort to peek into, make inroads, into languages and mental universes different from yours. Though the journey into them is a long one and it ain't easy going… the point is to keep going and going. You may not reach the status of a quadratic or cubic individual, but it's still possible to become more complex, spiritually richer person. Though without ever being able to become someone else.

Soul Travelling

Every step beyond one's own backyard is also a step inside, towards your soul. If my love of travelling isn't obvious by now, I am a very poor writer indeed. I should have no need to praise travel explicitly. But I have noticed one thing that may interest you. As you wander along the roads of this world, a long movie rolls out permanently in front of your eyes, hundreds and hundreds of frames. Some of them you filter out, some barely register and some you remember so well that if you close your eyes you can see and hear them widescreen-Panavision-Kodacolor-3D-Dolby stereo. It is because when you see such scenes the first time, in reality, you connect with them as a radio with a transmitter. You find yourself on the same wavelength, amplitude and frequencies in sync, the green magic eye of the old radio clears up and allows you to resonate. And you know that this is it, this is yours, this is what you immediately identify with.

It might be a certain redwood on a stony river bank at the bottom of King's Canyon, or a small campground in a pine forest in another canyon, dominated by a rock that, against the darkening sky, looks like a grizzly on its hind legs. It might be the flowing feminine curves of the prairie on the right bank of the Missouri river in South Dakota, or maybe even a certain stetson that you might wear if you go for hats at all. Through some mysterious alchemy you feel an affinity with some places, feeling comfortable around them, feeling at home around them, in them. Which doesn't mean you have to have that huge rock from Zion park or Niagara falls in your backyard.

You understand those places instinctively. They are yours. They have always been yours, waiting for you. Nobody can pull the wool over your eyes any more, hand you crap, mislead you, keep the secret from you. It feels a little bit as if those places speak your language, as if they were pre-destined to fill a little nook that you had made ready for them in your soul. The special place might be famous or maybe not. If it doesn't connect with something in you, despite all its fame, you may admire it, respect it, but you will not love it. Very often, you discover that your preconceived images, regardless of their source, were erroneous, false, distorted, or at least inexact. Now you are standing here and seeing with your *own* eyes and it's up to you to form your *own* opinion. This is the very moment for a peek inside your soul, as it is your soul that tunes up and colours your response. And this is the true beauty and glory of travelling.

* * * * * *

Mr O or Epilogue

We have almost reached the last page, dear reader. Just allow me one more thing. I need to add the other bookend to hold all these episodes together and prevent them from falling off the shelf. Besides, the ending should be symmetrical with the beginning, the prologue complemented by the epilogue.

After my Mom passed away, I travelled to Prague to settle the inheritance. Part of it was my Dad's archive. Part of that was seventeen vinyl LP records containing newer editions or recordings of his songs. I was impatient, eager to listen to them, so while the rest of the archive sailed on the cheap by boat, I paid premium to send the records the air mail.

Back home in London, I was looking forward to listening to the records. I waited a week – nothing. I waited a second week – nothing. I began to be nervous, imagining that the plane carrying those irreplaceable records had crashed, disappeared in the Bermuda triangle, was hijacked... I couldn't eat, I couldn't sleep. I was cursing under my breath all the time.

Then, one evening, the telephone rang. A complete stranger from Vancouver informed me, in a somewhat irritated tone, that Canada Post delivered to his home a parcel from an unfamiliar sender, containing some records in an unfamiliar language. He found my name in the parcel, and since he was able to obtain my phone number, he was calling to enquire if it might be mine and if so, what he should do with it. Of course I immediately sent that good man money to repack the records and send them my way. And of course the days following I couldn't restrain myself from name-calling, from piling curses in adult-only language on Canada Post or Canada Customs or whoever caused the mess.

When the records reached me, I understood. Despite all its governmental clout and power, and standard operating procedures, Canada Post and Canada Customs were innocent; they were helpless. On those records there were no less than three versions of *Going West Ain't Easy Going*. Do you see my point? Having been for so long banned and barred in Bohemia, the song could finally spread its wings and fly out into the wide world. Naturally, to be true to its name, it did all it could to fly as far West as possible, all the way to Vancouver. I think you will agree that facing such determination, no hapless postal or customs clerk stands a chance.

Well, thanks to the good people living in Canada, the recordings made it to me. Finally, I could place one on a turntable, let it spin and hum along with the singer: "Going West..."

Acknowledgements

The biggest thank you goes to Stan Dragland for editing this manuscript and for his unwavering long-term support of my writing career.

I thank Jean McKay for helping me to refine my vocabulary by suggesting the right words and idioms.

The photograph on the cover, Valley of Fire, Nevada, is by Kristy Massey, and I'm grateful for her kind permission to use it.

Thank you to Christine Mach of Double Q Printing for expertly designing the cover and interior of the book.

The lyrics quoted in the Prologue are from the song Je na Západ cesta dlouhá and are used with the permission of the copyright owner.

About the Author

Ivo Moravec was born in Prague, Czechoslovakia and educated as an industrial economist. Since his early twenties he has been developing a literary career parallel to his professional one, writing song lyrics, plays, TV scripts, and children's stories. When he found both his careers blocked for political reasons, he defected with his wife and son in 1983 from communist Czechoslovakia to Austria and from there immigrated to Canada. He settled in London, Ontario, and ultimately found a job on the assembly line at a Ford plant. After fifteen years in Canada he succeeded in reviving his writing career. In 1997 McClelland & Stewart published *Tightrope Passage, Along the Refugee Route to Canada*, an account of his defection and life in an Austrian refugee camp. After his retirement from Ford, he has worked as a ski instructor at the local ski hill. This experience is reflected in *Delirium Dives, Stories from the Ski Slopes*, published in 2015.

Ivo lives with his wife in London, Ontario.

www.ingramcontent.com/pod-product-compliance
Lightning Source LLC
Chambersburg PA
CBHW070613300426
44113CB00010B/1516